Creating a Classroom Culture That Supports the Common Core

Creating a Classroom Culture That Supports the Common Core

Teaching Questioning, Conversation Techniques, and Other Essential Skills

Bryan Harris

Routledge
Taylor & Francis Group

LONDON AND NEW YORK

First published 2014
by Routledge
711 Third Avenue, New York, NY 10017

And by Routledge
2 Park Square, Milton Park, Abingdon, Oxon OX14 4RN

Routledge is an imprint of the Taylor & Francis Group, an informa business

© 2014 Taylor & Francis

Library of Congress Cataloging-in-Publication Data

Harris, Bryan.
Creating a classroom culture that supports the common core : teaching questioning, conversation techniques, and other essential skills / Bryan Harris.
  pages cm
  Includes bibliographical references.
 1. Education—Standards—United States. 2. Education—Curricula—Standards—United States. 3. Classroom environment—United States. 4. Classroom management—United States. 5. Academic achievement—United States. I. Title.
  LB3060.83.H37 2013
  371.102'40973—dc23   2013034347

ISBN: 978-0-415-73535-3 (hbk)
ISBN: 978-0-415-73230-7 (pbk)
ISBN: 978-1-3158-4923-2 (ebk)

Typeset in Optima
by Apex CoVantage, LLC

Printed and bound in the United States of America by Publishers Graphics,
LLC on sustainably sourced paper.

Contents

Acknowledgments

As is the case with any book, the ideas and strategies assembled and described here are the result of the work of many individuals. Although my name appears as the author, this project could not have materialized without the assistance, the ideas, and the support of some amazing people. I am indebted to the following for helping this project become a reality.

My wife Becky and my sons Andrew and Jeremy are a total blast to live with. God has blessed me greatly and to say that I love these people wouldn't do justice to the honor and privilege I feel to be part of their lives.

The teachers, administrators, and staff of the Casa Grande Elementary School District have been integral to testing these ideas and providing feedback. I am grateful to work in an organization that constantly keeps student welfare and achievement at the center of all our conversations.

A unique group of instructional specialists, each of them extraordinary educators, have kept me on my toes and I am appreciative of their ideas and perspectives. Each of these people have made me a better educator: Lisa Dempsey, Leslie Kramer, Lisa Bradshaw, Cassie Goldberg, Andrea Munoz, Brandy Shuman, Sandra Schroeder, Margaret Rucker, and Carmen Rodriquez.

And finally, a special thank you to the outstanding team at Eye On Education. Bob Sickles, Lauren Davis, and Toby Gruber are a joy to work with and I am most appreciative of their patience, feedback, and perspective.

About the Author

Bryan Harris is the Director of Professional Development and Public Relations for the Casa Grande Elementary School District in Casa Grande, Arizona. In his 20+ year career in education, he has served as a middle school teacher, an instructional specialist, an elementary school principal, and a district-level administrator. He has a passion for helping educators find creative and effective ways to manage and engage students. His dynamic and practical presentations make him a sought after speaker and consultant. Annually, he presents to thousands of educators across the country on the topics of student engagement, classroom management, motivation, and brain-based learning. His first two books, *Battling Boredom* (Eye On Education, 2010) and *75 Quick and Easy Solutions to Common Classroom Disruptions* (Eye on Education, 2012) are considered some of the best resources available on the topics of student engagement and classroom management. He can be reached at www.bryan-harris.com.

Introduction

Back in late 2009, when I first starting hearing about the Common Core State Standards, I was a bit resistant to the idea of a national set of standards. I worried about the costs associated with realignment of curricula and services, the huge number of professional development hours staff would need to successfully implement the new standards, and I was concerned that the Common Core would result in an assortment of NCLB-type unintended consequences. Like educators all over the country, I thought to myself, "Here we go again. Well-meaning but naive politicians trying to improve schools through a top-down approach that will take an incredible amount of work but won't likely make much of a difference."

As I began to learn more about the Common Core, I slowly became convinced that, if done right, the Common Core has the potential to dramatically improve the quality of education for the nation's students. *If done right* seems to be the operative phrase here. Over the last few years, I have received a lot of questions about the Common Core and its potential impact. I recall one rather animated debate with an educator who questioned the need for the Common Core, "Will the Common Core really make a difference or will this just be another thing teachers have to do?"

This is the million dollar question—will the Common Core make a difference? As is the case with any educational innovation or initiative, the potential impact depends entirely upon the quality of implementation. If we only give lip service to the standards without any substantive change to what happens daily in classrooms, then the Common Core State Standards will be a miserable failure. However, *if done right,* the Common Core has the potential to positively change the education landscape and result in increased learning, achievement, and motivation for millions of students across the country.

What do I mean by *if done right?* First, we need to realize that standards alone are almost completely useless. While the Common Core State Standards do an excellent job of outlining the content and skills students need to possess to be college and career ready, they will not make up for bad teaching. What takes place in classrooms will likely have to change to meet these new standards. Without a corresponding shift in instructional strategies and methodologies, the power of the Common Core is lost. But the same can be said of any set of standards—be they local, statewide, national, or international—standards alone don't impact student achievement without an alignment between those standards and instructional practices.

Second, since classroom practice will need to be adjusted to meet the expectations of the Common Core, educators will need to ensure that the overall classroom organization, atmosphere, and culture, is crafted in a way that is conducive to the expectations of the Common Core. Upon the adoption of the Common Core by most states, teachers and leaders immediately went to work at aligning curricula, creating support documents, and updating assessments. While those are all valuable and necessary, less consideration has been given to the changes that will need to be made to the way classrooms are managed and the way students are engaged. Thus, the focus of *Creating a Classroom Culture That Supports the Common Core* is on how to set a foundation upon which teachers can build for successful implementation of the skills of the Common Core. *If done right* refers to giving the proper attention to both skill development and mastery of content.

Ensuring that students meet the expectations of the Common Core may require a shift in thinking for some educators. Traditionally, a "good" education was primarily defined by the amount of content an individual was able to master and utilize. For too long, content knowledge alone has been viewed as the ultimate goal of education. However, the Common Core places much more emphasis on the skills a student needs to master in order to be prepared for life after high school.

The Skills of the Common Core

From my perspective, the single most significant difference between the Common Core Standards and most previous versions of state standards is the emphasis placed on the development, refinement, and demonstration of student skills. Throughout the book, I will refer to skills as the verbs in the standards. When you take a close look at the Common Core Standards you'll notice the prominence of terms like *explain, critique, apply, represent, clarify, describe,* and *evaluate.* The nouns in the Common Core—the content students need to master—are really not all that different from most other sets of standards. For example, the math and language content a 3rd grader needs to know and master in the Common Core is essentially the same in the Common Core as it is in most versions of standards throughout the country. The difference, as I see it, is what students are to do with the content knowledge once it has been mastered.

Depending on your state, there has been some movement of content knowledge expectations between grade levels. While some of those grade-level shifts have received a lot of attention, they are not the most significant change teachers need to be prepared for. The biggest change is the emphasis on what students are to do with their content knowledge as reflected in the verbs utilized throughout the Common Core Standards. While standards have always included skills in the form of verbs, the Common Core takes the development of these skills to another level. A "good" education will be defined both by what a student knows as well as what they can do with what they know.

To highlight this shift towards the development of skills, take a close look at Figure I.1. This word cloud gives greater prominence to the verbs that appear more often in the Common Core Standards. The size of the font for each term indicates the frequency of that term. For example, Figure I.1 is a listing of the verbs found in the K-12 Reading Literature Standards of the Common Core. You'll notice that the verb *analyze* is the largest while terms like *refer, recognize,* and *retell* are much smaller. In fact, *analyze* appears over 20 times in this portion of the Standards while the terms *refer, recognize,* and *retell* appear 3 times or less. This helps to highlight the expectation that students become much more actively involved in manipulating content knowledge.

A greater emphasis on verbs or skills is not only to be found in the English Language Arts Standards of the Common Core. The Common Core Mathematics Standards are built on a set of eight expectations known as the Standards for Mathematical Practice. These eight statements describe the skills (or practices) of mathematically proficient students. The Mathematical Practices are described this way in the Common Core documents, "The Standards for Mathematical Practice describe varieties of expertise that mathematics educators at all levels should seek to develop in their students."

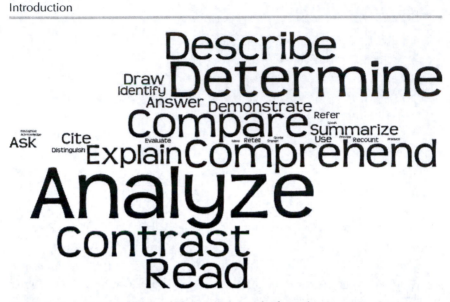

Figure I.1 Word Cloud Showing Key Verbs from the Common Core

As you'll see in Figure I.2, there is an expectation that students are deeply involved in the development of skills related to the mastery of math content knowledge.

Highlighting the need for skill development is not to imply that content knowledge is unimportant. A student cannot be expected to *reason, analyze, critique,* or *apply* knowledge they do not have. In other words, a student has to have some knowledge base upon which to apply those skills. Rather this approach is an attempt to bring back a sense of balance for students and teachers because content knowledge alone will not be sufficient if students are to be fully prepared to compete in a global 21st Century economy. Students need both a solid base of content knowledge and a set of transferable skills.

This balance between skills (verbs) and content knowledge (nouns) may likely be the most significant shift in thinking for us to consider. It might also be the least discussed issue as we prepare to fully implement the Common Core Standards. If content knowledge standards were the only issue, we'd likely have very little work to do to prepare our students to meet the expectations. However, the verbs used throughout the Common Core call for much more depth, much more student engagement, and much more complexity.

1. Make sense of problems and persevere in solving them.
2. Reason abstractly and quantitatively.
3. Construct viable arguments and critique the reasoning of others.
4. Model with mathematics.
5. Use appropriate tools strategically.
6. Attend to precision.
7. Look for and make use of structure.
8. Look for and express regularity in repeated reasoning.

(http://www.corestandards.org/Math/Practice)

Figure I.2 Standards for Mathematical Practice

This all leads to a very important question, "Are our schools ready to support the development of skills in addition to the mastery of content knowledge?" Traditionally, schools have been designed around the need to deliver a core set of content knowledge to all students. Therefore, we have created a system to deliver a set of facts and information related to math, reading, writing, science, social studies, etc. As previously stated, content related to these subjects is still important and will always be a priority. Of course we want our students to be literate and to have mastered a set of facts and information related to important topics. However, we also know that facts alone are not sufficient to be considered fully educated. Students need both—content knowledge and a set of skills that enable them *to do something* with that knowledge.

Design and Features of this Book

The focus of this book is to provide educators with the tools upon which to build a classroom foundation that supports both content knowledge and skill development. My assumption is that most classrooms are already designed for the delivery of content knowledge. While I also assume that many classrooms are designed to help students develop and refine skills, I know that the Common Core Standards are a game changer in this area. To be truly college and career ready, students will need to spend years mastering content and developing skills.

It is worthwhile to take a moment to note what this book is not intended to provide. It is not intended as a general guide to the Common Core. I will not provide background about the history of the Common Core nor will I offer a description of specific standards. We will not "deconstruct," "dig deeper," or "unwrap" any of the actual standards and I will not offer a tutorial on how to read the standards. My assumption is that teachers and leaders across the country have already begun the process of implementing the Common Core through alignment of curricula, the creation of support documents, and training staff in how to use the standards. While those are all valuable and necessary processes, they are beyond the scope of this book. This book is designed as a guide that helps to build the kind of classrooms where students learn content while developing skills. As a result, it is strategy-rich with a focus on easy-to-use tools that are effective at helping students and teachers meet the skill-focused expectations of the Common Core.

Chapter 1—*Creating a Classroom Culture That Supports the Common Core*—highlights the need to craft the overall classroom atmosphere in a way that supports the development of skills. This chapter includes a specific focus on the need to develop a classroom culture where students are willing to take risks. Because the development and refinement of skills requires that students step outside their comfort zones, an environment that supports risk-taking is essential.

Chapter 2—*Managing Behavior in the Common Core Classroom*—tackles the important issue of classroom management. Knowing that skill development requires a lot of student activity and participation, this chapter centers on the assumption that traditional discipline and management methods will not be sufficient to meet the expectations of the Common Core. Rather, the best thing teachers can do is teach students how to regulate their own behavior.

Chapter 3—*Rigor in the Common Core Classroom*—offers teachers specific tools and ideas for how to increase the likelihood that students learn content in a deeper, more meaningful way. This chapter will include an overview of definitions related to rigor and will offer teachers a glimpse into some of the skills that students will need to develop in order to be prepared to compete in a global economy.

Chapter 4—*Questioning in the Common Core Classroom*—addresses the art of questioning and how it relates to the development of student skills. Questioning is perhaps the oldest and one of the most effective instructional strategies teachers have at their disposal. This chapter will offer four characteristics of effective teacher questioning in addition to numerous easy-to-use strategies.

Chapter 5—*Critical Thinking in the Common Core Classroom*—deals with the often-misunderstood skill of critical thinking. Often-cited as lacking in American students, this ability is absolutely necessary if students are to meet the grade-level expectations of the Common Core as well as be ready for life post high school. This chapter will provide definitions, a connection between critical thinking and the Common Core, and specific classroom applications.

Chapter 6—*Academic Conversations in the Common Core*—will address the need for classrooms to become places where students talk *a lot* about academic topics in order to both master content and develop skills. If students are to meet the demands of the Common Core and be college and career ready, they need to be able to communicate and talk about their knowledge. Therefore, this chapter will provide the strategies and tools to help teachers increase academically-focused student talk.

At the end of each chapter I offer two sections that are intended to assist educators with the application and extension of the ideas presented in that chapter. The **Reflection Questions** will focus on the content and strategies presented in that chapter and are designed to assist with the application of strategies and concepts. The **Extend Your Knowledge** section includes citations, notes, research, and additional information on topics that were addressed in that chapter.

1 | Creating a Classroom Culture That Supports the Common Core

Key Idea

If students are to exhibit the skills of the Common Core, the classroom culture, environment, and atmosphere must support the development of those skills. This necessitates specific attention, time, and focus. A supportive classroom culture requires that teachers embody respect in their daily interactions with students and that they spend time teaching the specific skills that will lead to student success. With a focused and positive classroom culture, students are more willing to take the risks necessary to build skills and deepen content knowledge.

Creating the Environment—Two Principles

As teachers, our job is to create, or craft, the learning environment for our students. Make no mistake, the classroom environment is either intentionally created by the teacher or it *gets* created by other factors including student personalities, class size, or the availability of resources and support. Either way, the classroom environment has a large impact on the development of student skills, attitudes, and mastery of content. The following two principles are foundational elements for creating the kind of classroom environment that will support the development of Common Core skills.

Principle #1—Embody Respect

Classrooms where students thrive are built upon respect and trust. Respectful environments and relationships serve as the foundation for students to build skills and expand their content knowledge. Disrespectful environments destroy trust and any willingness a student may have to take a risk. Concepts related to psychological safety suggest that students must first believe, often through concrete examples, that they are safe from teasing, ridicule, embarrassment, or shame. Richard Lavoie, in his book *The Motivation Breakthrough,* points to the connection between safety and motivation:

> Children simply cannot learn if they feel unsafe, threatened, or insecure. The classroom environment must be tolerant, accepting, welcoming, and secure. One of the primary roles of the teacher is to protect the physical and emotional well-being of the students. Motivation cannot exist in an environment where children feel or fear embarrassment, humiliation, intimidation, or isolation. (p. 95)

In essence, we need to *be* the things we expect of our students. Respectfulness needs to permeate every interaction we have with students. Here are three ways to embody respect.

Build Positive Relationships

Everything we do in the classroom runs on the currency of relationships. The idea of currency is used here specifically to point out that relationships are not constant or stagnant, they change and evolve. Just as our bank accounts fluctuate every day based on expenses and income, relationships are fluid and ever changing. Once we establish positive relationships with students, we must always work to build on that foundation. There are times when you'll ask students to do something they've not done before or to do something that is uncomfortable. In those situations, you'll need to draw upon the currency that you've built up. If there is nothing "in the bank" it will be a challenge to get a student to take a risk. The book *Quantum Teaching* uses the term "affinity" to define the closeness, affection, and admiration that teachers should seek to develop with their students. Although we may get students to follow procedures or rules through the use of threat, intimidation, or negative interactions, true learning and risk taking require personal connections that result from trust. Rapport is built when individuals listen to each other, value each other's background, and genuinely enjoy being around each other. When students know that the teacher truly likes them, that they care about them as a person, they are more willing to engage in the learning tasks and challenges in the classroom. Here are four easy ways to build relationships with students.

- **Ask questions**—Get to know the likes, dislikes, interests, hobbies, and outside-of-school activities of your students. Many teachers provide questionnaires or surveys at the beginning of the year. Use that information to build relationships with students.

- **Make positive contact with home**—Relationships need to be built with families as well as with students. Use positive phone calls, emails, notes, postcards, and home visits to open the lines of communication. As educators, we need to realize that there is a lot we can learn from parents about how to best educate their children. Plus, every parent loves to hear good things about their children. When we spend the time to make the connection with families, it pays off in the classroom.

- **Share a laugh**—Humor is a powerful tool in the classroom. It can relieve tension, liven up a boring lesson, focus student attention, and help create an environment where students want to be. When people share a genuine laugh together, it strengthens their bond, connection, and commitment to each other. Use stories, knock-knock jokes, funny pictures, or personal incidents as an opportunity to laugh. Make a commitment to spend just a few minutes each day laughing with your students.

- **Share something personal**—Most students want to know something about their teachers. While they won't likely be all that interested in a teacher's resume or career accomplishments, they still want to know a little bit about the teacher's background, interests, passions, etc. Offer age-appropriate stories, artifacts, personal experiences, or pictures so students get an understanding of who you are as a teacher as well as who you are as a person.

Avoid Negativity and Sarcasm

Nothing will destroy trust or a positive classroom environment faster than negative or sarcastic comments. As will be outlined and repeated throughout this book, students need to be willing to take a risk in order to develop the skills necessary for success in the Common Core. As teachers, we simply cannot embody respect while at the same time infuse our daily interactions with negativity and sarcasm. Just as humor can open up and expand a relationship, sarcasm can close it off and destroy trust very quickly. Although negativity and sarcasm often appear together, they are not the same. Sarcasm is typically defined as negative humor and has no place in the classroom, even with older children. It should not be used as a teaching or classroom management tool because it destroys trust instead of building it. One of the challenges when working with older students is that they often recognize sarcasm as humor and will laugh. They may even provide sarcastic comments back to the teacher or to other students. Regardless, it is not a technique that builds positive relationships because students will be less likely to be vulnerable if they know they may be on the receiving end of a sarcastic comment.

When considering if your interactions with students are sarcastic, think about intent. If the intention of the comment or statement is to ridicule, point out errors or faults, or to mock a behavior, it might come across as sarcastic. Both sarcasm and negative comments often result from frustration or lack of student compliance. For example, the following response to a student's cell phone ringing in class would be sarcastic, "Uh, EXCUSE ME. I guess the rules don't apply to you. Why are you so important that you need your phone on? Are you expecting a call from your girlfriend? Wait, you don't have a girlfriend, do you?" To gauge if your daily interactions are often negative or sarcastic, you have three valuable resources. First, ask your students if there are times when your comments, jokes, or interactions come across as negative, mean, or impolite. In some cases, you may need to apologize to students that you have offended. Second, seek the advice of a trusted colleague. Talk to a fellow educator who is willing to provide an accurate assessment of your interactions with students. Ask your colleague to observe your classroom with the goal of providing feedback about how you interact with students. Finally, consider audio recording a class. An audio recording has several benefits over a video recording. It is much easier to set up and, unlike a video, there is no worry about getting focused on the wrong things. The sole focus should be on the verbal interactions that take place in the classroom. When used as a personal reflection tool, it can provide valuable insights into the classroom environment. (Some schools or districts may have a policy providing guidelines for the use of audio recording so consult with an administrator prior to using this strategy.)

Model Behaviors

We are always modeling behaviors, deliberate or not, positive or negative, we are always modeling. In the context of embodying respect, we need to model the positive behaviors we expect of our students. If we want students to be patient and forgiving, we need to be patient and forgiving. If we expect students to say "please" and "thank you" we need to do the same. Our profession is unique in the sense that our customers, our students, are always watching us. They watch how we handle frustration, how we handle good news, how we deal with unexpected events, how we deal with deadlines, how we organize our own materials . . . they watch everything. Knowing that their eyes are always on us, we have a duty to demonstrate, in our daily behaviors, what we expect of students. If we do not, we run the risk of (rightfully so) being labeled a hypocrite. In addition to ensuring that our personal behaviors are congruent with our expectations of others, we can use strategies such as Think Alouds (see p. 7) to help students understand how we think, process, and come to conclusions when faced with problems or challenges.

Principle #2—Teach Skills

It can be frustrating to attempt to teach a group of students who don't know how to think critically, how to resolve conflicts, how construct an argument, or how to critique ideas. However, consider the fact that if students came to us as they *should* be, there would be no reason for teachers in the first place. When our students lack the necessary skills to be successful in the classroom, it is our duty to teach them those skills. We need to teach them how to think critically, how to resolve conflicts, and how to critique ideas. Remember that the Common Core is a game-changer in the sense that the focus is on both content knowledge and skills. The skills are those verbs in the standards that require action based on content knowledge. If we expect students to demonstrate knowledge, we need to teach them both the knowledge and how to demonstrate it. For some, this will require a shift in thinking away from solely focusing on content mastery. Content mastery alone, as will be outlined in Chapter 3 will not be sufficient in preparing our students for the challenges of the next century.

Outlined here are four general strategies that make skill development fun, interactive, and effective.

Looks Like, Sounds Like, Feels Like

This strategy offers teachers and students alike the chance to clarify expectations and state them in concrete terms so that everyone has a clear understanding of what the skill looks like, what it sounds like, and what it feels like. This is particularly useful for helping students understand abstract skills such as evaluate or persevere. Children are implored to *think critically, describe thoroughly,* or *compare ideas* only to find the teacher's expectations are very different from their own. Nowhere is this conflict more evident than in the classroom. Teachers often tell students to behave in terms that are abstract and open to interpretation. Provide students with a handout that has three columns: one labeled Looks Like, another labeled Sounds Like, and another labeled Feels Like. At the top of the sheet, list *one* specific behavior or skill, such as *engaging in a collaborative discussion*. In partnership with the student(s), brainstorm the specific behaviors that you expect when students are in that situation. The first two columns—Looks Like and Sounds Like—focus on external behaviors that can be seen and measured by both the student and the teacher. The Feels Like column lists how students would expect to feel if they were meeting expectations and demonstrating that skill.

Photographic Evidence

Many students respond well to visual images that provide support, examples, and evidence of expected appropriate behavior. This strategy uses images and pictures to demonstrate what a skill might look like. Gather images and pictures that demonstrate expected classroom behaviors. For example, what does the mathematical practice of *attend to precision* look like? Compile images and pictures in a folder or envelope, or tape them onto the surface of a desk for individual students. Include a brief description or title for each photograph, such as "When tackling a tough problem." Some teachers use plastic picture inserts, the type that come in wallets, and give one to each student. When providing direction, support, or guidance to students, refer to the Photographic Evidence in addition to providing verbal redirections or reprimands.

Fish Bowl

Just as we observe fish in a bowl, this strategy allows students to see, hear, and observe what other students think about a concept, question, or scenario. As an analogy, tell students that fish in a bowl live in an environment where everyone can see what they are doing. When we watch fish in a bowl, we observe how they live. Although we can't see what fish think, we can observe how they act. Place two or three students in chairs in the center of the group and give them a topic or question to discuss. Tell students that they will have a discussion for approximately two minutes. When cued, the students in the Fish Bowl start to have a discussion centered on the topic or prompt provided by the teacher. Students can provide answers, give examples, or state opinions. The students on the outside are instructed to follow along with the conversation because they may be asked to join the conversation at any given time. When appropriate, the teacher asks the students in the Fish Bowl to pause and then selects a student to enter the Fish Bowl and replace one of the members. The newest member of the Fish Bowl then continues the discussion. This strategy is powerful because it allows students to see the skill in action.

Think Alouds

Although often used as a reading comprehension strategy, a Think Aloud serves as a great tool to help students understand *the process* that an individual goes through while completing a task, answering a question, or resolving a conflict. Teachers often begin a Think Aloud by explaining the scenario or problem and then verbally walking students through their thinking. Basically, we are verbalizing that internal dialog that goes on within each of us as we attempt to solve a problem. Much like the Fish Bowl, this strategy supports skill development because it allows students to hear what the skill looks like in action. However, this strategy does not need to only be used by teachers. When students think aloud, either directly to the teacher or with a partner, it allows them to practice and experience the skill.

The Importance of Risk Taking

Think about the concept of risk. Some people like to take risks, some people avoid them at all costs. As adults, we understand the critical connection between risk and reward. With risk comes the possibility of reward but with risk also comes the possibility of failure. In the classroom, we ask students to take risks on a daily basis. We ask them to think differently, to make connections they've not made before, to talk about things they've never talked about, and to act in ways they've never acted before. In order to do those things, they need to be willing to take a risk and try something new. This is, in fact, the essence of learning and growth. When teachers embody respect and take the time to teach skills students are more likely to take the risks necessary to meet the expectations of the Common Core. The trusting, respectful classroom where skills are taught is the foundation upon which students will take those risks.

Risk taking is also a skill that will be expected when students enter college or begin their careers. In fact, some of the most celebrated, high-profile companies such as Google and 3M, expect their employees to take risks and "think outside the box". However, merely *requiring* students to take a risk will rarely work unless there are structures and supports that promote the taking of risks. As Figure 1.1 shows, the purpose of embodying respect and

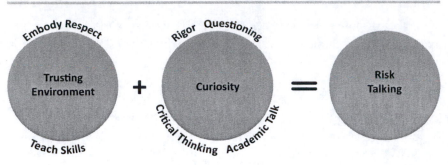

Figure 1.1 Creating a Trusting Environment

teaching skills is to create a trusting environment where students know that their basic needs will be met. Once students believe they are in a trusting, secure classroom, we must work to boost their curiosity. We do this by considering the role of rigor in the classroom learning. Rigor will be expanded upon in Chapter 3. We also pique the curiosity of our students by employing effective questioning strategies (Chapter 4), by infusing critical thinking into all aspects of the classroom (Chapter 5), and by allowing students the opportunity to talk about what they are learning (Chapter 6).

Four Ways to Promote Risk Taking

The willingness to take a risk is an essential skill for academic success. However, once again, merely telling students to try harder or take a risk isn't going to work. There are, however, several concrete strategies that can promote this concept and help students take a step towards taking a risk. Outlined here are four ways that will help to teach students about the importance of taking a risk.

#1—Normalize Error

If we are honest, in most classrooms failure is something to be avoided. We teach so that students master content and are "right" in their thinking. Students learn early on that the goal of school is to repeat the correct answer; the goal is to be right. Culturally we are taught to be ashamed of our mistakes and hide them from other people. However, true learning involves a lot of mistakes and reflection on mistakes is a valuable source of learning. In fact, it is the truly wise among us who admit their errors, faults, and mistakes and make a commitment to better themselves. If students are to be willing to take a risk, they need to understand the role of error in learning. Making an error is not bad, it is not something to be avoided, and it should not be embarrassing. In fact, errors and mistakes are an indication that risks are being taken. In discussions with students, talk about how errors are a normal part of learning and that if no errors are being made, it might be a sign that the work is too easy. Errors merely provide an opportunity to learn. In the classroom, this means that we should normalize error in our daily interactions with students. Error, as strange as it may sound, should be a part of the classroom culture. John Hattie, in his book *Visible Learning,* points out that:

> School leaders and teachers need to create school, staffroom, and classroom environments where error is welcome as a learning opportunity, where discarding incorrect knowledge and understandings is welcomed, and where participants feels safe to learn, re-learn, and explore knowledge and understanding.

When we make error a normal part of the classroom, we help students to understand that progress is rarely a straight line.

#2—Teach Students How to Struggle

With risk taking comes struggle. It may sound like a contradiction, but there needs to be some struggle on the path to success. Our students need to understand that the road to success is typically paved with setbacks, obstacles, and struggles. Success and struggle actually go hand in hand but, just as our culture doesn't always support the notion of admitting mistakes and errors, it rarely acknowledges the positive aspects of struggle. The idea of struggle can be found clearly in the mathematical practice of *make sense of problems and persevere in solving them.* In order to persevere, students need to know the how, the why, and the ultimate goal of struggle. Here are four guidelines for teaching students how to struggle.

Explain Why
Struggle should have a purpose. Struggling just to struggle is frustrating. There needs to be a sense of movement towards a payoff, reward, or outcome. When

working with students, be clear when a struggle or obstacle may be encountered and help them to understand how that struggle may lead to a goal or desired outcome. Connect the struggle directly to the learning objective. When monitoring lessons, you may find yourself saying things like, "Right now I'm going to let you work on this on your own. I'm going to let you wrestle with this problem for a couple minutes on your own. I'm going to help you in a couple of minutes, but right now I want you to tackle this on your own." Some teachers have incorporated specific vernacular in their classrooms to help students develop this habit. They refer to *wrestle time, struggle time,* or *deep thinking time.*

Share Stories and Examples

Stories are among our most powerful instructional strategies and they serve as a very influential way to get across important messages to students. As teachers, we can use stories, illustrations, and examples to highlight how struggle has helped us. We should be willing to share personal examples of how we have dealt with adversity and what we have learned from it.

Model

Teachers should use classroom time to model, in real time, the process they use to deal with challenges and dilemmas. Using Think Alouds and other direct strategies, we should walk our students through the steps needed to persevere and work through challenges. Statements like, "When I got to this point in the problem, I felt like giving up. But I kept going and I tried this step instead. I'm glad I did because . . ." In order to persist through a struggle students need stamina. Students learn mental stamina by observing effective models and by practicing those skills themselves.

Debrief and Show Progress

When students have persisted and worked their way through challenges or obstacles, it is important to take time to debrief with them and show them how that struggle has helped them to succeed. Don't view struggle time as an opportunity to be "mean" or "firm" or to "put them in their place." Remember that struggle has to do with academic growth, personal reflection, and learning. Don't deny students the opportunity to reflect on their journey. Allow them the joy of discovering the depth of their internal strength but remember that struggle must be differentiated for the student. Not all students can handle the same kinds of struggles or for the same amounts of time.

#3—Show How Failure Helps

There are some things that failure teaches you that success cannot. When we are faced with our shortcomings and failures, it can force us to take a hard look in the mirror in order to reflect and consider changes. Facing failure, much like accepting that errors are normal and that struggle can be a good thing, requires a shift in thinking for many of our students. This shift in thinking can be found in the quote attributed to Thomas Edison in reference to his work to perfect the light bulb, "I have not failed 700 times. I have not failed once. I have succeeded in proving that those 700 ways will not work. When I have eliminated the ways that will not work, I will find the way that will work." In the process of learning and taking risks, we all face failure and hardships. Our students need to know that personal mistakes, those things that may seem like failures, are often the best source of information for future growth. We can, and should, learn from our mistakes. However, many traditional classrooms are set up to prevent mistakes from students.

If students enter the world beyond school having never experienced nor dealt with failure, we are doing them a disservice. From a broader perspective, students need an internal set of skills and character traits that reflect a resiliency in the face of hardship. Some educators have used the term "grit" to refer to the ability to face failure without giving up. That is, for their ultimate future success as an adult, they need to have the mindset that they will not give up in the face of failure. As a concrete way to help students understand that failure can be a good thing, share real-world examples of people and organizations that have faced initial failure and yet thrived. Share stories about personalities like J.K. Rowling, Walt Disney, Dr. Seuss, and Steve Jobs so students have concrete models and examples of individuals who have thrived despite initial failures.

#4—Celebrate Success

In encouraging students to take a risk, we cannot forget about the power and potential of celebrating success. At times, classrooms can be so focused on the end result of grades, assessments, labels, and academic achievement that we forget to take the time to celebrate the small victories that our students experience. If we devote classroom time and energy towards teaching a skill or content, then we ought to celebrate the success of our students, large and small. Here are two ways to help celebrate success:

Compliments and Congratulations

Everyone appreciates a genuine compliment and recognition of a job well done. When the teacher takes the time to regularly provide positive statements in the form of Compliments and Congratulations, wonderful things can happen in the classroom climate and in the behavior of individual students. A compliment on a personal attribute such as work ethic or congratulations on the achievement of certain goals can be motivating to many children. In addition to a boost in motivation, Compliments and Congratulations tell the child that his or her efforts or characteristics are noticed and valued.

Communication with Home

Teachers can communicate with home in a variety of ways. Phone calls, e-mails, text messages, handwritten notes, postcards, newsletters, Web sites, and personal conversations are all effective tools that help to connect with families. All parents like to hear good things about their children and when we take the time to tell parents of the successes of their children, it can increase student motivation and the levels of home support schools receive.

Summary

The importance of a positive and supportive classroom environment cannot be understated as it relates to the development and refinement of student skills. As teachers embody respect and commit to teaching skills, it sets the foundation for students to take risks. Risk taking is essential because the Common Core calls for students to be much more active in the development, management, and refinement of their knowledge.

Reflection Questions

1. In the book *50 Ways to Improve Student Behavior,* authors Annette Breaux and Todd Whitaker suggest that half of all student behavior problems can be solved if teachers and students laugh more together. In what ways could you incorporate humor into your classroom?

2. Do you find yourself sometimes being sarcastic with your students? If so, what tools or reminders could you use to help eliminate this habit?

3. The importance of communication with home was highlighted twice in this chapter. What methods do you use to regularly and positively communicate with families?

4. What personal stories can you share with your students that would help them to understand that error, struggle, and failure can be beneficial?

5. Students need to be willing to take a risk in order to develop skills. What other strategies have you tried that help students to take a risk?

Extend Your Knowledge

- The willingness to take a risk is highly correlated to personal motivation but not all students are motivated by the same thing. To learn more about concepts related to motivation, read Richard Lavoie's excellent book *The Motivation Breakthrough—6 Secrets to Turning on the Tuned-Out Child.*

- For more ideas about how to build positive relationships with students, read *Connecting with Students* by Allen Mendler. It outlines dozens of easy to use, fun, and effective ways to build trust and open lines of communication.

- It is much easier to embody respect with students who are polite, respectful, and compliant. The hard part comes when dealing with challenging or difficult students. For strategies to deal with difficult student behavior, read *75 Quick and Easy Solutions to Common Classroom Disruptions* by Bryan Harris and Cassandra Goldberg.

- To learn more about Think Alouds, read *Teaching Reading in the Content Areas* by Rachel Billmeyer and Mary Lee Barton for definitions, examples, and tips.

- To learn more about the concept of normalizing error, read the John Hattie's book, *Visible Learning.* An excellent strategy to normalize error, called *My Favorite No,* is highlighted on www.teachingchannel.org.

Managing Behavior in the Common Core Classroom

Key Idea

If students are to exhibit the skills of the Common Core, they need to learn to regulate their own behavior. Self-regulation is a skill to be learned, practiced, and refined and includes the ability to guide and direct one's behavior, attitude, and attentional focus. If we want a well-run, efficient, and positive classroom where students consistently demonstrate Common Core skills, the best thing we can do is teach students how to regulate and control their own behavior.

What is Self-Regulation?

In recent years, cognitive and social scientists have renewed their interest in studying factors related to an individual's ability to regulate their own behavior. A review of the literature and research related to self-regulation will reveal a range of concepts, terms, and ideas associated with the ability to control and direct one's actions, thoughts, and emotions. Different researchers and scientists study different facets or variations of this broad concept referred to as self-regulation. Depending on the philosophical bent of the researcher or the specific question being studied, you'll find related terms like self-control, self-direction, self-monitoring, self-discipline, self-management, and self-motivation.

Sometimes referred to as an executive function process in the brain, the capacity to control and direct one's behavior has obvious and significant implications for classroom teachers. As educators our experience tells us that students who are unable to regulate their behaviors, their emotions, or their thinking processes are at a greater risk of inappropriate behavior. In other words, they get in trouble in school more often. Out of necessity for the good of our students, we have an obligation to teach students what self-regulation is, how it can be developed, and why it is important for their long-term success in school and life.

For our purposes here, as it relates to success in the classroom and the development of Common Core skills, we will refer to self-regulation simply as the ability to control one's behavior and make choices that are in their own and in other's long-term best interest. It includes a combination of skills, habits, and thinking patterns that allow an individual to successfully navigate the temptations and challenges of life in order to make correct and appropriate decisions. The ability to self-regulate needs to be overtly taught, practiced, and refined over time. Additionally, it requires specific time in the daily school curriculum because the Common Core challenges educators to consider the long-term development of students, not just whether they can pass yearly, state-mandated tests. The good news for educators and parents everywhere is that self-control can be learned. Later in the chapter I'll outline methods and strategies that will help students develop this critical ability.

How Serious Is Self-Regulation?

In the late 1960s, psychologist Walter Mischel conducted a series of experiments that later became known as the Marshmallow Test. Mischel wanted to determine the factors that influenced decision-making, attention, and willpower so he devised a series of experiments where individuals were asked to delay gratification in the short term for a promise of a larger reward in the long term. Initially conducted with preschoolers at Stanford University's Bing Nursery School, the tests involved measuring young children's ability to wait for a treat such as a marshmallow, pretzel, or cookie. In the experiments, children would be escorted into a room and asked to sit at a table upon which sat the treat. They were told that they had a choice; they could either eat the treat immediately or wait a few minutes and get an additional one. Mischel wanted to study the differences between those children who could delay immediate gratification and those who could not.

The findings from those early studies resulted in some surprising and relevant facts for classroom teachers. By following students as they progressed through their school career and into adulthood, Mischel found that the children who were able to delay gratification and wait for a second treat did better in school, had more positive peer relationships, and were less likely to experience behavioral difficulties. Students who succumbed to the desire for immediate gratification—those who took the initial treat without waiting—also had some common characteristics including more reported levels of impulsivity, more discipline problems, and lower grades (Mischel, Shoda, & Rodriguez, 1989).

The Marshmallow Test has been replicated thousands of times all over the world and researchers have studied variations including the impact of different types of treats, the differences between younger students and older students, the effect of groupings on the outcome of the test, and even the differences in siblings and twins. The different variations consistently show the same results. Those students who are able to delay immediate gratification stand a much greater chance of being successful in school and in life.

Terrie Moffitt, a Duke University psychologist and researcher has also considered the role of self-control in an individual's short-term and long-term success in life. In one of the most seminal studies on the topic, she studied data from 1000 people from their birth to their early 30s. After controlling for factors including IQ and socio-economic, Moffitt and her colleagues found that individuals with lower levels of self-control were at significant deficits. Those individuals reported greater dependence on drugs and alcohol, increased financial problems including lower credit scores, greater rates of sexually transmitted diseases, and increased likelihood of involvement in crime (Moffitt, et al., 2011).

Yet, despite the startling information about the impact of poor self-regulation skills on a student's immediate and future prospects, the work of Mischel, Moffitt, and many others has found that self-regulation can be developed. For educators, this is both encouraging news and an immediate challenge. If our students are to be successful in developing and demonstrating the skills of the Common Core, they must learn how to regulate their own behavior. If they must learn it, we must teach it. As Mischel points out, just because a child eats the marshmallow doesn't mean they are doomed. The good news is that self-regulation can be learned and the earlier we begin teaching students how to control their own behavior, the better our classrooms will be. Quite simply, the ability to regulate one's own behavior is the best predictor of success in school and life (Baumeister & Tierney, 2012). The earlier we can help students learn self-regulation, the better their overall school experience will be and the greater chance they will develop into students who are college and career ready. The evidence is clear—self-regulation skills serve as a reliable predictor of success in school and life.

What Works? What Doesn't?

Think about the world we live in. There are temptations and choices, good and bad, at every turn. On a daily basis, we are faced with options about what to eat, how to spend time and money, and how to react to disappointment. The ability to consider long-term benefits over short-term pleasures or solutions is extremely important. If we can deny ourselves the pleasure of an expensive meal and instead invest that money for retirement, we are making a vital decision in our best interest for the long term. It is the same with students in the classroom; those students who can deny themselves the temporary pleasure of off-task behavior in favor of focusing on a learning task have an advantage in school, learning, and ultimately in life.

While it's not always easy, self-regulation can be increased through practice and reflection. Like many cognitive and emotional skills, self-regulation can be compared to a muscle—the more it gets used, the stronger it becomes. What then, is effective at helping students build those skills? C. M. Charles, author of *Building Classroom Discipline* (2010) states that, "Techniques for supporting self-control are low-keyed. They are not forceful, aggressive, or punitive but aim at helping students help themselves." That is the key here—techniques that are "low-keyed" and focus on "helping students help themselves"—are the ones that are more likely to help students develop into the kind of self-regulated, reflective individuals that we desire. First, let's take a brief look at those practices that are *not* likely to produce self-regulation skills in students.

Classroom systems that rely on rewards, punishments, and strict external control do little to teach students how to control their own behavior (Kohn, 1999). Student names written on the board, charts displaying names of students with good and bad behavior, marbles in a jar, team points, competitions, and the like rely solely on the teacher as the external judge of appropriate behavior. Under such systems, children are not required (and sometimes never given a chance) to make choices or reflect upon their own behavior. In those environments students don't learn to regulate themselves because their behavior is always regulated for them. At best, those systems provide a consistent source (albeit a fairly poor one) of feedback regarding how the teacher is currently judging their progress or lack of progress.

Those systems may reinforce students who already exhibit the ability to self-regulate but they do not teach skills to students who are lacking.

For a student to truly learn how to regulate and direct their own behavior, they need to be given opportunities to make choices, to reflect on their progress, and to make mistakes in a safe environment free of public ridicule. To put it more bluntly, systems that rely on strict external control will not teach an individual the skills or thinking patterns they need in order to be successful when those controls are removed. And that, after all, is one of our most important responsibilities as classroom teachers; to teach students how to be successful learners when they are no longer with us.

In addition to ensuring that we have a classroom management system in place that encourages and teaches self-regulation, we need to consider our own communication styles and the specific interactions we have with students who are lacking skills. Students with poor self-regulation abilities will not develop an understanding of appropriate behaviors and choices solely through nagging, reminders, and verbal reprimands. One of the challenges we have as teachers is remembering, and truly internalizing, the principle that the students with the greatest behavioral and academic challenges are the ones who need us the most.

A classroom reality is this—students who are low in self-regulation skills are more likely to have discipline problems. As such, if we are honest, they are the students most of us least enjoy interacting with. This is a real conundrum for educators. Those students who are high in self-regulation are typically better liked by their teacher and their peers (Reif, 2003). They are easier to get along with and easier to teach. The low self-regulation students make our jobs more difficult while the high self-regulation students make it easier. Is it any wonder, then, that the high-in-self-regulation students do better in school? They not only have the advantage of some internal skills and abilities, they also get more positive feedback, praise, and direction from their teachers. But the students that need us the most, the ones that need the very best teachers, are the ones who need help in developing self-regulation skills.

Five Ways to Teach Self-Regulation

Since self-regulation is a skill that needs to be learned, we have an obligation as educators to teach students the specific methods, strategies, and techniques that will allow them to be successful. Merely telling a student to exhibit self-control is pointless unless the student has the resources, knowledge, and skills to do it. Outlined here are five general approaches, grounded in the research, that are useful and effective and helping students develop self-regulation skills.

Support the Brain

Although the brain is only about 2% of a person's total body weight it uses about 20% of the body's energy consumption. It's a bit of an energy hog taking more than its share of resources from the body. Glucose, the brain's primary energy source, is depleted whenever we engage is tasks that require attentiveness, willpower, or self-control. When we undertake tasks that require executive functions glucose levels in the brain drop almost immediately. In other words, glucose is literally the *fuel for thought* in the brain. Without the proper nutrition and fuel in the brain, it can be very difficult, if not impossible, to perform tasks related to self-regulation. Since the brain needs glucose in order to perform tasks related to self-regulation, as educators we need to consider the ways we can assist the brain in maintaining the proper levels. Here are two easy ways to help students maintain useful glucose levels in the brain:

- **Allow students to eat and drink**—The brain gets its fuel the same way the rest of the body does—through what we eat and drink. To maintain proper glucose levels, the body needs the right nutrition. Healthy snacks including complex carbohydrates like fruits, grains, and nuts provide the brain with a steady supply of glucose. Avoid simple carbohydrates like sugary treats and sodas that tend to quickly spike glucose levels only to have them crash soon after. While students should regularly drink water for other brain-healthy reasons, water alone doesn't impact glucose levels. When it appears that students may be struggling to focus and attend to tasks, consider the need for the brain to get the right levels of nutrition. In other words, the brain has to be fueled up and ready before students can exhibit willpower or self-control.

- **Increase physical movement**—For many years, the traditional thinking was that students would be more likely to focus and maintain self-control when they are in a sedentary, low-movement environment. While this assumption may still be prominent, it goes directly against what we know about what the brain needs. In addition to releasing glucose stored in the liver, physical movement increases attention, raises metabolism levels, and generally raises alertness levels (Jensen, 2005). When students are struggling to maintain self-control, one of the best things we can do is offer them a stretch break, a walk around the classroom, or a chance to participate in activities like ball-toss games.

Make it Fun

Learning self-control doesn't have to be painful and it shouldn't feel like a chore. In fact, if we approach the development of self-regulation skills from the perspective that students have to suffer—that they have to feel pain— we are likely going to be facing very reluctant students. Positive emotions like anticipation, laughter, fun, joy, and amusement help to place students in the proper state to consider how they can develop or refine their skills. In other words, positive emotions are more likely to open doors and create an opportunity to reflect and grow. While it is true that some lessons in life need to be learned the hard way, there is much we can do to prepare students to face situations where they'll need to demonstrate self-control. Fun activities such as the ones described below offer students the chance to experience a positive pay off when they are successful while limiting the negative consequences they experience when not completely successful.

- **Incorporate games**—Traditional childhood games like Simon Says, Concentration, Follow the Leader, and Telephone are great ways to help students practice focus, attention, and self-regulation. They are fun, highly engaging for students, and can easily incorporate academic topics.

- **Use role-playing**—There is a reason professional training programs rely heavily on the strategy of role play. Pilots, lawyers, and surgeons all rely on this practice in order to refine their skills and get feedback about their progress. Situations in which students role play real-life situations are extremely valuable because they allow students the chance to think through options and challenges before they occur.

- **Offer scenarios and intriguing questions**—We all enjoy the challenge of thinking through unique or novel situations and most of us enjoy solving problems, especially those that belong to someone else. Challenge students to consider how they could respond to certain situations they'll likely face. Do this through stories, what if-type questions, or video clips in order to offer students the chance to consider their response to a scenario or question.

Improve Working Memory

Sometimes referred to as short-term memory, working memory has been described as the brain's Post-it note. It is the process in the brain that holds a small amount of transitory information for a short period of time until the brain decides what to do with it. The information stored in working memory drives executive brain functions like planning, problem solving, organizing, and paying attention. To be successful in the classroom, students need to have efficient working memories because there are many times they are asked to remember directions, key ideas, facts, examples, procedures, or keep time limits "in mind" while they complete tasks. In fact, a good working memory has been found to be a better predictor of school success than IQ (Alloway & Alloway, 2010). Students with inefficient working memories will struggle to recall the directions and steps necessary to be successful in the classroom. Think about the number of times we become frustrated when a student says, "What are we supposed to do now?" when we've literally given them the directions just moments before. There may be many reasons students seek help in such situations but when we can help them improve working memory—when we can help train their brains to better access and utilize such information—the better they will do in our classrooms and ultimately in life. The good news is that, like the other skills we've discussed throughout this chapter, working memory can be improved. Below are a few examples of strategies that can help students to improve working memory.

- **Use Spot the Difference activities**—Tasks requiring students to locate differences between pictures or objects can strengthen working memory. Provide students with two seemingly identical images or objects and ask them to locate the differences. Daily newspapers have been offering Spot the Difference cartoons for decades and there are literally thousands of free images, puzzles, and games available for free online.

- **How many can you recall?**—Place a variety of common classroom or household objects on a table and cover them with a towel. Depending on the age of the students, the number of items can range from 10 to 30. Tell students that they will be given 30 seconds to look at all the items with the goal of memorizing everything they see on the table. After 30 seconds of looking, studying, and memorizing, cover the items back up with the towel and ask students to write down everything they can recall.

- **Externalize information**—Consider all the types of information that are externalized for our benefit as adults. We benefit from traffic signs that remind us of speed limits, clocks that keep us on time, and auditory alerts from our phones that remind us of appointments. These external reminders help to guide our behavior by providing us with information we can act upon. In the classroom, students also benefit from having some information externalized for them. Provide visual cues for things like directions, time limits, due dates, key facts or vocabulary, and lesson objectives.

- **Repeat and verbalize information**—Consistently ask students to verbalize and repeat information related to the tasks they are being asked to complete. Avoid asking questions such as, "Are there any questions?" or "Does everyone understand?" and instead require students to speak about the steps they need to take in order to be successful. The process of verbalizing and speaking about tasks can support working memory and it helps when students hear from their peers about their plans as well.

- **Play games**—Most games require participants to hold and process pieces of information in working memory. The ability of the brain to hold and manipulate multiple pieces of information is necessary to win games such as 20 Questions, Hangman, Concentration, Chess, as well as traditional board games like Monopoly.

Do a Room Check

The physical environment of the classroom can have a big impact on a student's ability to focus and exhibit self-control. Consider for a minute the current condition of your classroom. Think about the placement of desks and furniture, the location of pencil sharpeners, word walls, or projectors, and the general state of the classroom in terms of organization and flow. Is it neat, tidy, and organized or cluttered, messy, and overly-stimulating? Some students, particularly those low in self-regulation, are sensitive to what Eric Jensen (2012) refers to as "hot cues". Those are the things in the environment that trigger a response in the brain and become very difficult to ignore. In other words, the condition of our classrooms may make it difficult to focus and practice self-control. Recall back to the Marshmallow tests conducted by Walter Mischel. The marshmallows were the hot stimulus; those were the things calling out for attention. Children who were able to distract themselves away from the marshmallows were more likely to delay gratification and earn a second treat. Many classrooms are full of "marshmallows" and other hot stimuli that are just calling out for attention. The point is, the physical work environment has an impact on a person's ability to focus. This is true for adults as well as for children. So, do a room check and consider removing clutter, objects, or other items that may be overly distracting to students.

Boost positive internal dialogue

Roy Baumeister and John Tierney, authors of *Willpower: Rediscovering the Greatest Human Strength* state that, "At its core, the capacity for self-control is essentially the ability to change yourself." Although external factors or conditions may prompt us to consider change, ultimately all lasting change comes from within. The ability to change is partially conditional upon the types of internal dialogues and conversations we have with ourselves. We all have an internal voice that we talk to that helps us to rehearse situations, consider how we might react to a scenario, or to help determine next steps when planning. After all, haven't each of us spent time rehearsing or practicing how we might respond to a difficult conversation? We are faced with choices about the types of internal conversations we will allow. Will they primarily be positive ones that focus on our abilities, choices, and strengths or will they be negative ones that focus on what we are unable to do? Some students who struggle with self-regulation may have negative internal dialogues that can be difficult to ignore. How I think about myself, what I tell myself, and what words I use to internally describe my abilities will be directly related to my willingness to exhibit self-regulation when it is needed. Since the internal conversations we have with ourselves are learned from external sources, there are some strategies that we can use as educators to help boost positive self-talk.

- **Create and track goals**—Goals, particularly those that are self-created, help the brain to prioritize focus and attention. In partnership with students, generate short-term goals that focus on achievable targets where they can feel successful. Provide them with checklists so they can see progress and ask them to regularly monitor progress in order to make adjustments or to celebrate accomplishments.

- **Provide feedback**—All students require feedback about their progress, growth, and achievement in order to be successful. Jane Pollock, author of *Feedback: The Hinge That Joins Teaching and Learning*, says that feedback is the hinge upon which almost all learning rotates. That is, feedback is central to personal growth and our job as teachers is to ensure that students receive the kind of feedback that will benefit them the most. Students who struggle with negative internal conversations will benefit greatly from positive, specific feedback that is focused on their abilities, strengths, and accomplishments. Since part of the goal is to help rewire or reframe some negative internal thoughts, we can help by providing positive feedback through questions, statements, and by celebrating their successes.

- **Model it**—The importance of modeling cannot be understated. By watching us, students learn how to handle frustrations, what to do when they meet unexpected challenges, and how to interact with people. In Chapter 1 we discussed the importance of modeling as it relates to the principle of embodying respect. In that chapter, I also described the strategy of Think Alouds in helping students develop skills. Those same ideas are relevant here as well because students need concrete representations of positive self talk and how it can lead to greater levels of self-regulation.

Summary

If students are to exhibit the skills of the Common Core—if they are to be set up for success post-high school—they need the ability to regulate their own behavior. Self-regulation, the ability to direct and control behavior for one's long-term best interest, is necessary for success in school and life. Since self-regulation is a skill to be learned, it must be taught and given specific time and attention in the school day. In fact, teaching self-regulation may be the best gift we can give to our students.

Reflection Questions

1. Fred Jones, author of *Tools for Teaching,* states that nagging is one of the primary classroom management tools used by teachers. He also says it is typically a waste of time. Do you find yourself providing a lot of verbal reminders (nagging) about off-task behavior? What procedures could be refined or replaced to address this?

2. In the section that discussed What Works? What Doesn't? I stated that systems that rely on strict external control including a reliance on rewards and punishments do little to develop self-regulation skills. Note that I specifically used the term punishment, not consequence. What is your understanding of the difference between a punishment and a consequence as it relates to developing self-regulation skills?

3. In regards to teaching students the skills of self-regulation, there are often questions about the role of the family and parents. "Shouldn't parents be teaching these things? Why is it the responsibility of the school?" While those questions have validity, consider the issue from a practical perspective. Attempting to teach academic concepts to students with little self-control is not only frustrating for both the student and the teacher; it is likely to be an exercise in futility. The fact is that self-control leads to academic achievement.

4. Have you ever said to yourself, "We don't have time for fun. We have too many objectives and too much content to cover."? To make something fun, in and of itself, is not the goal. The goal is the mastery of academic content and skills. Fun is a factor that can open the door and provide a motivating aspect so that students will be more willing to tackle academic topics. How can you incorporate more fun into your classroom?

5. The chapter focused on building self-regulation skills in students. How will you speak with your students about what self-regulation is, why they need to develop it, and how it will benefit them in your class?

Extend Your Knowledge

- Much has been written about social-emotional learning and the importance of educating the whole child. For an excellent resource that includes specific lessons, reproducibles, and activities for training the brain look into the MindUp curriculum created by The Hawn Foundation—www.thehawnfoundation.org.

- A true must-read and the best book currently available that outlines the psychology and application of concepts related to self-control is *Willpower: Rediscovering the Greatest Human Strength* by Roy Baumeister and John Tierney.

- For an excellent summary of the work of Walter Mischel as well as modern day variations of the Marshmallow Test, read *The New Yorker* magazine article titled "Don't—the Secret of Self-Control" by Jonah Lehrer (2009).

- The development of self-regulation ability is gradual. It takes time, practice, and effort to develop the kinds of skills necessary to be successful in school and life. For an excellent overview of the development of self-regulation skills in young children read the article "Developing Young Children's Self-Regulation through Everyday Experiences" by Ida Rose Florez printed in *Young Children* (July 2011).

- To learn more about how the brain works, read Eric Jensen's popular book *Teaching with the Brain in Mind*. For an excellent source of specific brain-based lessons to use with students, check out *Brain-Powered Strategies to Engage All Learners* by LaVonna Roth.

Rigor in the Common Core Classroom

Key Idea

If students are to exhibit the skills of the Common Core, they need to develop and apply those skills in a way that is rigorous. Rigor is less about what we teach or even how we present information. Rigor is about *what students do;* it is about what they experience and how they apply their knowledge and understanding. Rigorous tasks and learning experiences are important because they help to prepare students to be college and career ready.

What is Rigor?

If you were to look up rigor in the dictionary, you'll find that most of the words and ideas associated with it are negative. Merriam-Webster uses terms like harshness, inflexibility, strictness, rigidity, and even cruelty to define rigor. Needless to say, those are not ideas we want associated with our efforts to educate children. In the context of classroom instruction and the Common Core, rigor refers to how students apply knowledge, think critically, and explore connections between concepts and ideas.

As will be explored later in the chapter, rigor focuses on depth of understanding and application of skills. Rigorous classrooms are focused on what students do with information and learning as they strive towards mastery of content. Rigor is important because the Common Core Standards require students to be much more active in their own learning and in their own development of skills. From this perspective, active engagement on the part of students is not merely centered on participating in the classroom activities designed by the teacher. True engagement in a rigorous task or process involves personal commitment, curiosity, and self-direction. Rigorous learning is one in which students are expected to master and apply skills and knowledge in personally meaningful ways. In a rigorous environment, students reflect on their knowledge in order to discover connections to other ideas and to other content areas. Rigor requires that students think critically, solve relevant problems, and actively demonstrate their knowledge in order to develop deep understanding. When rigor is defined from this perspective it is a very positive thing for students because they become active *participants* instead of passive *recipients* of learning. The Common Core Standards require that students think critically, that they solve problems, that they make connections between content areas, and that they apply what they know. Quite simply, rigorous learning opportunities provide a way for students to meet the expectations of the Common Core.

Concepts Associated with Rigor

Several concepts and ideas appear consistently in the literature relating to rigor. A closer look at these ideas is helpful when constructing an understanding of how rigor should be applied in a classroom setting.

Application & Demonstration in a
High-Expectation Environment

A classroom environment where students are expected to apply and demonstrate knowledge and understanding is a hallmark of a rigor. Classroom tasks and activities alone however, are not sufficient in getting to the depth required to be truly rigorous. What we ask of students is that they master content knowledge with the goal of applying and demonstrating that knowledge in meaningful ways. This involves holding high expectations for all students and offering all students the support necessary to be truly successful by Common Core guidelines. Barbara Blackburn, author of *Rigor is NOT a Four-Letter Word,* speaks to the connection between rigor and high expectations, "Rigor is creating an environment in which each student is expected to learn at high levels, each student is supported so he or she can achieve at high levels, and each student demonstrates learning at high levels."

In this context, rigor can be viewed as philosophy or belief about teaching that we hold as educators. As professionals, we must hold ourselves to high expectations as much as we do our students. The design of the learning environment and the creation of learning opportunities must reflect rigor if students are to be successful at developing the skills that will enable them to be successful post high school. In order to meet the expectations of the Common Core, we may have to set aside old ways of doing things; we may need to re-invent ourselves and expand our repertoire of lessons, units, and resources. Instruction in which students are drilled on basic facts in order to pass tests will not prepare our students for the 21st Century.

Reflection & Self-Direction

When students are involved in a rigorous task or assignment, they will be required to reflect on their learning and progress. They will be given the time, the support structures, and encouragement necessary to consider what they've learned, how they've learned it, and what they still need to learn in order to meet goals and demonstrate their understanding. In a rigorous classroom, students show self-direction because they can see the connection between assignments and learning goals. Self-direction involves making choices about what is learned, how it is learned, and how it will be demonstrated. As was discussed in Chapter 2, students need to be overtly taught how to be self-directed and should be provided with specific models and support structures that allow them to be successful.

Rigor and the ability to direct one's own learning should not be viewed as something only to be done by older students. At a very young age, children must be exposed to the essentials of rigor—challenge, mastery, reflection, and application. The International Center for Leadership in Education says that rigor is, "learning in which students demonstrate a thorough, in-depth mastery of challenging tasks to develop cognitive skills through reflective thought, analysis, problem-solving, evaluation, or creativity. Rigorous learning can occur at any school grade and in any subject."

Critical Thinking & Depth of Understanding

For decades, since the start of the standards movement, teachers have complained, rightfully so, that standards are "a mile wide and an inch deep". Standards have often been criticized as vague, irrelevant to the needs of students, and politically motivated. While some of these arguments are valid, the good news is that the Common Core Standards have addressed many of those shortcomings. Primarily, the Common Core aims to get students to think critically and deeply about important concepts and ideas that will build the skills necessary to be college and career ready. The Common Core requires that students demonstrate mastery of fewer topics but in more in-depth ways stressing evidence, communication, and application.

David Coleman, one of the authors of the Common Core Standards, has stated that the Common Core is "focused and concentrated on what matters most". This focus on thinking, depth, and integration of ideas will require that we organize our classroom instruction and curricular resources differ-ently. If we require critical thinking and depth of understanding, we must devote the time necessary to teach students how to do those things. Again, this may require that we set aside traditional ways of organizing our schools and classrooms so that students are given the time and resources to think critically and develop depth of understanding.

Concepts Not Associated with Rigor

Just as a review of the concepts associated with rigor is helpful in under-standing classroom application, a closer look at practices not associated with rigor is helpful because the contrast can help us determine how class-room experiences can be adjusted and changed. Essentially, this is a list of what rigor is *not*. Rigor has many, sometimes competing, definitions that confuse the conversation and can make it difficult to determine what is essential to meeting the needs of students. Therefore, this short list is intended as a way to reflect on classroom practice with the goal of getting to truly rigorous learning that will meet the expectations of the Common Core.

Harder Work & More Work

Recall that rigor focuses on depth of understanding, application of knowl-edge and skills, and personal reflection on learning and growth. While some educators may want to claim that they are rigorous because they pro-vide a lot of very difficult, challenging, and complex work, they may in fact be denying their students the joy and satisfaction of experiencing rigor. Recall also that rigor is about what students experience, not necessarily what teachers do. While additional, more complex tasks may be needed for some students to experience rigor, making a blanket statement such as "I'm a rig-orous teacher because I provide a lot of homework" or "I'm more rigorous than other teachers because I teach above grade level" merely demonstrates that the person doesn't truly understand rigor. Just because something is hard, doesn't mean it is rigorous. In fact, tasks and assignments that are too difficult prevent students from experiencing the depth, application, and reflection that are necessary for rigor. Cris Tovani, author of several books on reading, including *I Read It, But I Don't Get It*, compares the terms hard and rigor and explains it this way, "there is a fine line between having a rigorous classroom and a hard one in terms of student success. Here is what I learned: Rigor invites engagement. Hard repels it."

Consider the issue of homework for a moment. This topic, hotly debated in recent years, often comes up during a discussion of rigor. Some teachers, feeling pressured by the need to "raise standards" have increased the amount of assigned homework to even the youngest of students. Without going into the merits and drawbacks of homework, examine the differences between these two homework assignments and how they relate to the concept of rigor:

> Homework assignment A—Complete 50 long-division math problems on a worksheet. Homework assignment B—Complete 2 long-division math problems and explain, in writing, your thinking process as you solved each one. Then talk with a parent, teacher, older student, or an adult about how long-division is used in real life. Be prepared to share examples in class.

Rigidity & Being "Tough" on Students

We've established that the traditional dictionary definitions of rigor are not applicable for classroom application. Harshness, rigidity, and a "life is tough—figure it out" mentality should not be part of the conversation. In order for students to have rigorous experiences, they need to be provided the appropriate support and guidance to create meaningful, lasting learning.

Recall that in Chapter 1 we discussed the importance of risk taking as it relates to the development of Common Core skills. Students rarely take risks unless they feel comfortable, safe, and valued by their teacher and by their peers. Therefore, as educators, it is our job to ensure that students are provided with the type of environment in which they experience specialized and differentiated support, instruction, and feedback. Just as hard doesn't equal rigor, neither does toughness or rigidity. In fact, as educators, we need to be more flexible and understanding because students will experience rigor in many different ways.

Coverage

The problem of superficial coverage of vast amounts of content has historically not served our students well. Not only has the coverage mentality failed our students it has frustrated teachers, parents, and employers as well. Standards are to be learned, not covered. When a teacher responds that they are "covering" the standards, it may be a clue that they may not be providing the depth and application that is necessary in the Common Core.

Additionally, it may be helpful to reframe the discussion from "I teach the standards" to "My students learn the standards". The entire focus, after all, in a rigorous environment is on what students do with the information they have learned. Teaching focuses on the actions of the teacher; learning focuses on the actions of the student. The Oregon Small Schools Initiative summed it up well, "Schools can demand rigorous intellectual work from students only if they give up the goal of superficially covering as much content as possible."

Tony Wagner's Seven Survival Skills

Tony Wagner gained international attention with the publication of the books *The Global Achievement Gap* and *Creating Innovators*. As a Harvard University professor much of his work centers on helping educators and schools create the types of learning experiences and support systems that will help prepare students for the 21st Century. Wagner's framework is helpful here because it forces us to step back and look at the demands that will be placed on our students once they leave school since the ultimate goal of the Common Core Standards is to prepare students to be college and career ready. In addition to mastery of content knowledge, Wagner believes these skills are absolutely necessary for students to thrive in the 21st Century global economy.

1. **Critical Thinking and Problem Solving**—As will be discussed more in Chapter 5, critical thinking is foundational to the skills students need once they leave school. The ability to think critically in order to solve problems and make decisions is so extremely important to employers that it consistently shows up in surveys examining the deficits and needs of recent college graduates. As educators, we need to provide opportunities for students to think and apply knowledge from the very earliest grades.

2. **Collaboration and Leadership**—In order to be successful post high school, particularly in an increasingly global market, students need to have the ability to collaborate with a wide range of diverse personalities. Collaboration involves the ability to listen, the ability to negotiate, the ability to compromise, and the ability to make decisions for the good of the organization. Collaboration and leadership are linked because students need to know how to exert influence and persuade peers regardless of formal leadership titles or positions. This is what employers want and need—individuals who can collaborate and lead in order to solve problems.

3. **Agility and Adaptability**—In the new global economy, change is a constant. Unfortunately, most schools and classrooms are designed for stability and same-ness. This uniformity of approach to teaching and learning will not prepare our students for success post high school. As a result, we need to provide opportunities in which students are able to practice and experience cognitive and emotional flexibility. They need to be immersed in learning environments in which they practice adapting to changing conditions, expectations, and scenarios. In essence, we need to help prepare them to live in an ever-changing world. Our challenge is doing so in an education system that often defies change.

4. **Initiative and Entrepreneurship**—Rigorous learning tasks, ones in which students care about the problems and seek to dig deeply into the learning, are more likely to produce a sense of initiative, growth, and the development of new ideas. School systems that stress compliance and "good" behavior may be directly at odds with the need for students to develop an entrepreneurial spirit. While schools often diminish or outright discourage opposing viewpoints or disparate thinking, those are the very things that may be of the most value as students enter the workforce.

5. **Effective Oral and Written Communication**—The ability to effectively communicate one's ideas, thoughts, and opinions is the foundation of a good education and is central to the Common Core. As evidenced by the proliferation of remedial reading and writing courses for college freshmen, we have not done an adequate job at the K-12 level of preparing our students for the demands of post high school life when it comes to communicating. This is partially due to the fact that we often focus more on content mastery and utilize a sit-and-get approach to teaching

that requires very little communication from students. Rigorous learning opportunities are more likely to produce authentic reasons for students to develop these valuable communication skills.

6. **Accessing and Analyzing Information**—Traditional teaching and learning relies on only a very few sources of information—namely the teacher and a textbook. However, the world is full of sources of information and our students sometimes have a difficult time navigating the complex, often conflicting views of vast amounts of information. In order for our students to be successful once they leave the system, they need to not only be able to access appropriate sources of information but they need to be able to analyze that information for bias, error, and credibility.

7. **Curiosity and Imagination**—A compliance-based classroom—one in which students are primarily the passive recipients of "teaching" and where they are expected to accept what the teacher says without question—will not prepare students for the demands of the 21st Century. In order for students to succeed and thrive, they need to be curious about their world, they need to ask questions and imagine possibilities, and they need to be placed in a system where they are expected to be actively involved in creating new ideas and imagining possibilities.

Rigorous learning opportunities are more likely to help students develop the survival skills described by Wagner. With these skills in mind, we can contrast rigorous learning tasks with traditional ones. In order for our students to develop those skills and truly be college and career ready, they need to have learning experiences that are more likely to produce them. As evidenced by the lack of skills of many of our high school graduates, traditional learning tasks fail to develop these fundamental skills. Wagner (2008) addresses the conflict in this way:

> To teach and test the skills that our students need, we must first redefine excellent instruction. It is not a checklist of teacher behaviors and a model lesson that covers content standards. It is working with colleagues to ensure that all students master the skills they need to succeed as lifelong learners, workers, and citizens. I have yet to talk to a recent graduate, college teacher, community leader, or business leader who said that not knowing enough academic content was a problem. In my interviews, everyone stressed the importance of critical thinking, communication skills, and collaboration.

Practices that Promote Rigor

Because rigor is that which is experienced by students, this section will outline those teaching practices that are *likely* to promote a rigorous experience. That is, they are practices that teachers could utilize in order to increase the likelihood that students would deepen their understanding, apply knowledge across content areas, and reflect on their learning. I use the term practices here instead of strategies for a specific reason. We typically think of strategies in terms of the specific, discreet tactic that a teacher utilizes to produce a desired outcome. An instructional practice however, is a broad term that can encompass many different strategies. For example, in Chapter 4 I describe the practice of questioning as it relates to the Common Core. In that chapter are ten specific strategies that can be used in the practice of questioning. With that in mind, below are some instructional practices that are likely to promote and increase rigor.

Barbara Blackburn, in the book *Rigor is NOT a Four-Letter Word,* uses rigor as an acronym to describe five practices that help to promote rigor:

- **Raise the Level of Content**—An important thing to remember when determining what content to teach is the fact that most of our students are capable of much more than we realize. Utilize grade-level standards, curricular maps, and the like as a starting point for students, not the end point.

- **Increase Complexity**—Rigorous learning experiences require students to demonstrate and apply knowledge and skills; they don't focus solely on acquisition of content knowledge. Much of what students are asked to do in traditional learning involves solving problems or completing assignments, but few of them require deep, critical thinking of complex issues.

- **Give Appropriate Support and Guidance**—For students to experience rigor, they need support, guidance, and feedback that is specific to their unique needs, questions, and concerns. Expecting students to demonstrate deep understanding without the right support is futile.

- **Open Your Focus**—Students are much more likely to experience rigor when teachers shift from a narrow set of expectations and instructional practices to more open-ended ones. Inherent in having an open focus is allowing choice and options in what students learn and how they demonstrate knowledge.

- **Raise Expectations**—Raising expectations starts with the assumption that students are capable (and willing given the right support) of tackling complex problems and making intelligent connections between ideas. Raising expectations is a reminder for us to hold high expectations for ourselves as well as for our students.

In addition to those practices described by Blackburn, I would suggest that the following are also likely to engage students in rigorous experiences in which they can practice and develop the skills necessary to be college and career ready:

- **Creativity**—Students have an innate desire to express their creativity and individuality. Unfortunately, because of an obsession with standardized testing, many schools have significantly reduced opportunities for the arts. When a student is involved in a creative task, whether it be a performance art, a visual art, or a literary one, they are more likely to address complex issues, make connections between content areas, and to reflect on their own learning.

- **Projects**—Whether you engage in a formal project-based learning framework or not, projects that require students to research a question or determine a solution to a problem are likely to encourage the types of behaviors we wish to see demonstrated. To be college and career ready, students will be expected to complete long-range, real-world projects that provide solutions to real problems.

- **Authentic, real-world problems**—Many of the problems we present to students, as well as some traditional instructional methods, are disconnected from real life. That is, they only appear in school and primarily serve the needs of the adults in the school. When problems, scenarios, and questions are taken from the real world, students are more likely to dive into rigorous experiences.

- **Reciprocal teaching**—As an instructional method, reciprocal teaching has been around for decades. Sometimes referred to as peer teaching and often a foundation in cooperative learning strategies, it can be a powerful way for students to experience rigor. In order to teach a concept to another person, one must have a depth of knowledge, an ability to communicate important ideas, and the ability to adjust to meet the needs of the learner.

Practices that Don't Promote Rigor

When it comes to devoting the resources and energy required to create rigorous learning opportunities for students, I'm often asked about time. I frequently hear something to the effect of, "I don't have the time to do all these extra things." My response is typically, "You're right. If you attempt to do everything you've always done, you won't have the time." As an analogy, imagine you want to be healthier so you seek the advice of a dietician. The dietician outlines recommendations for a healthier life starting with the food you consume and gives the recommendation to purchase a gym membership. Looking over the recommendations and suggestions you respond with, "I can't afford to buy a gym membership and all this healthy food is going to cost a fortune." If you continue to live life as you always have *and* attempt to comply with the dieticians suggestions, you are right—you probably can't afford it. The only way you can afford to make those changes is to stop doing certain things. In relation to classroom practice, in order to make "room" for rigor, certain practices will need to cease. It makes sense, therefore, to reconsider some traditional (and ineffective) practices that are not likely to produce the kinds of skills we need from our students.

- **Copying**—Once a hallmark of traditional instruction, many teachers have come to understand the limitations of asking students to copy, word-for-word, information from a board or another source such as a dictionary. At best, copying notes and recreating information provides students with a source of information on which to reflect and refer. However, copying is not engagement and there are much more valuable ways students could spend their time.

- **Extended lectures**—Also once a hallmark of traditional education, lectures as an instructional strategy have become a hot topic in recent years. Typically done with the whole group, at best lectures provide all students with the same information at the same time, with the same pace, utilizing the same modality. However, not all students need the same information at the same time in the same modality. Lectures typically offer little or no differentiation and they require no real engagement on the part of the students. As an alternative, provide mini-lectures of 5–7 minutes on topics related directly to the needs of the students and challenge them to consider application of ideas and connections across content areas.

- **Whole group "discussions"**—Discussions are not a bad thing and whole group instruction is necessary at times. However, what we often refer to as a group discussion is really just a brief, closed question and answer session between the teacher and a few select students. Traditional class "discussions" rarely engage more than a few students at a time. Rather, use whole group discussions sparingly in order to get students interested and thinking about a topic and then transition to small-group and paired discussions that focus on deeper questions and application of knowledge.

- **Worksheets and packets**—Worksheets, packet work, and a reliance on solo, independent work will not prepare students for the reality of the demands of college and career. In the real world, learning rarely involves completing piles of paperwork in a solo environment. It is true that there are times when we must complete paperwork (job applications, filing taxes, etc.) but those times are typically unrelated to learning and mastery of content. At best, a reliance on worksheets and packets will get students to focus on quiet, independent work but they will not help students master the skills necessary to thrive in the 21st Century.

Summary

Rigorous learning experiences offer students a chance to develop and refine the skills they'll need to succeed and thrive in the 21st Century. As educators, we have an obligation to provide learning opportunities where students develop a deep understanding of complex, real-world issues. Part of this obligation may require that we let go of traditional teaching techniques because, although they may help students learn basic content knowledge, they are insufficient at helping students create deep, connected, and lasting learning.

Reflection Questions

1. What conversations would you expect to hear between students if they were involved in a rigorous project or discussion?

2. Most traditional teaching techniques are teacher-dependent meaning that the learning and activities are solely dependent upon the teacher for the content and the process. Rigorous learning experiences require more activities that are student-dependent. That is, students will need to be self-directed and make their own connections, applications, and reflections. What tools or techniques do you use that require students to be more dependent on themselves for learning?

3. What connections and similarities can you identify between rigor and differentiated instruction?

4. Since rigor is experienced by the learner, what formative feedback strategies could you utilize to gauge the interest and progress of your students?

5. Robyn Jackson, author of numerous books including *Never Work Harder than Your Students* says that, "Basically, academic rigor is helping students to think for themselves." Reflect back on a lesson you taught recently. What strategies, tools, or techniques did you utilize to get students to think for themselves?

Extend Your Knowledge

- To learn more about Tony Wagner's Seven Survival Skills, check out his website at www.tonywagner.com.

- The topic of homework has been hotly debated in recent years. Some researchers claim there is no connection between the amount of homework given and academic achievement. Others claim that homework is valuable because it helps to build discipline and study habits. Still others speak to homework's negative effects on families. Some great books on the topic are: *The Homework Myth* by Alfie Kohn, *The Battle Over Homework* by Harris Cooper, and *The Case Against Homework* by Sara Bennett and Nancy Kalish.

- One of the most significant and user-friendly books on the topic of rigor is *Rigor is NOT a Four-Letter Word* by Barbara Blackburn. In this book you'll find a multitude of tools, tips, and ideas for implementing rigor.

- If you'd like to dig a little deeper into specific tools and frameworks related to rigor, read about the Rigor/Relevance Framework™ created by the International Center for Leadership in Education. Combing concepts from Bloom's Taxonomy and the work of Willard Daggett, this framework provides an excellent tool to examine the interplay of curriculum, instruction, and assessment.

- Text complexity is a term that is often discussed in relation to the Common Core English Language Arts standards. To learn more about this topic, read *Text Complexity—Raising Rigor in Reading* by Douglas Fisher, Nancy Frey, and Diane Lapp.

4 | Questioning in the Common Core Classroom

Key Idea

If students are to exhibit the skills of the Common Core, they need the ability to communicate ideas, thoughts, insights, and knowledge. Teachers can support the development of communication skills through the utilization of effective questioning strategies. Listening, speaking, thinking, and communication skills are all enhanced when teachers employ specific questioning practices that require students to respond to prompts, think critically about information, and communicate knowledge and ideas.

Questioning in the Classroom

Asking questions is at the very heart of what we do as teachers. The role of *teacher as questioner* is as old as teaching itself and the research on questioning is filled with the positive effects that result when teachers employ effective questioning strategies. Few topics in the field of education have been more widely researched or supported as effective at increasing student achievement and engagement. Consider just some of what we know about questioning:

- Questioning is second only to teacher talk as the most-used teaching strategy in classrooms. Teachers spend up to 50% of instructional time posing questions (Black, 2001; Cotton, 1988).
- Teachers ask between 300 and 400 questions per day (Brualdi, 1998).
- Most of the questions asked by teachers are at the lowest cognitive levels—basic recall of facts and knowledge (Walsh & Sattes, 2005).

- Low-level, surface-type questions lead to low-level, surface-type answers. Higher-order questions lead to deeper understanding by students (Hattie, 2008).

- Asking questions that are beyond a student's level of understanding or ability can lead to "downshifting"; an emotional response that occurs when a student is fearful of being ridiculed (Gregory & Chapman, 2002).

As educators, we would be wise to spend time sharpening our skills in this area. Questioning, aside from being prevalent in classrooms, is effective at achieving many of the goals of the Common Core State Standards. In addition, all teachers—from novices to veterans, can improve on their questioning skills. Regardless of how good you currently are at crafting, asking, and responding to questions, you can always get better. Consider what Walsh and Sattes (2005) say about the power of teacher questions, "If questions are vehicles for thought, then the questioning process determines *who* will go along for the ride. *Teacher questioning behaviors affect which students learn and how much.*" Clearly, our actions in relation to questioning have a big impact on our students and their ultimate ability to demonstrate the skills of the Common Core.

Questioning and the Common Core

A review of the Common Core State Standards reveals the importance of questioning—both for the teacher and the student. As teachers, it is our responsibility to craft questions and utilize strategies that require students to think deeply and process information. For students, they have the responsibility, again as reflected in the standards, to respond to questions from others, to collaborate during discussions, and to ask questions of their own.

The Speaking and Listening Standards rely heavily on a student's ability to interact with peers in collaborative discussions. A close look at the standards reveals the skills students must demonstrate in order to meet the College and Career Readiness Anchor Standards. At the K-5 level, students must *ask and answer questions, participate in collaborative conversations with diverse partners, build on other's talk, ask for clarification*, and *engage effectively in a range of collaborative discussions*. These foundational skills are expanded in the middle school and high school levels to include the expectation that students *elaborate on ideas, reflect on the perspectives of others, follow rules for collegial discussions, pose questions that elicit elaboration,* and *propel conversations by posing and responding to questions.* Questioning—both by the teacher and by the student—serves as an important and necessary strategy to help students develop and demonstrate these skills.

The importance of questioning, and the communication skills it develops, can be found throughout all content area standards as well. In addition to the Speaking and Listening Standards mentioned above, references to questioning can be found overtly and implicitly throughout the English Language Arts (ELA) Standards and the Math Standards. For example, the standard for Reading for Informational Text (RI) at grade 1 states that students must *ask and answer questions about key details in a text.* This expectation is expanded as the grades progress to include more sophisticated and complicated skills.

The Standards for Mathematical Practice, which describe the behaviors of mathematically proficient students, also rely heavily on a teacher's ability to ask questions and a student's ability to communicate understanding. Consider just one of the practices—*construct viable arguments and critique the reasoning of others.* In order for students to demonstrate this ability, the teacher must ask specific, probing questions to uncover understanding and help students to communicate that understanding in a logical way. Additionally, in order for students to critique the ideas of others, they must generate and respond to relevant questions.

Knowing that questioning, both by the student and by the teacher, is a foundational skill of the Common Core, teachers should spend time reflecting on their practice and making adjustments to best meet the needs of their students. Questioning certainly is good, sound educational practice, but it is also essential to helping students meet the expectations of the Common Core.

Four Characteristics of Effective Questioning

Much has been written and researched about the characteristics of effective questioning. Researchers have looked at issues such as the structure of questions, the length and complexity of questions, teacher training in developing and implementing questioning strategies, the use of wait time, the effect of feedback on student responses, and the relationship between student responses and extrinsic rewards, to name a few. An exhaustive list of all the characteristics of effective questioning would require volumes to summarize and might be too lengthy to be of use to busy educators. For our purposes here, as it relates to the Common Core, I have described four characteristics, supported by the research, that help students to meet the communication expectations of the Common Core.

Pre-Plan Questions

Great teaching and exemplary learning don't happen by chance. As educators, we need to be intentional about the questions we ask our students and the strategies we employ to engage them in processing those questions. Intentionality is the key. We need to devote time to planning which specific questions we intend to ask during various parts of a lesson or activity. In the process of lesson planning, we should write down those questions and not rely solely on our memory, the questions listed in a textbook, or spur of the moment responses to student actions. This is perhaps the most important message of the entire chapter—we must pre-plan our questions. After all, we want our students to be thoughtful in response to our questions (that is, we want them to *plan* their responses) so we should devote the time and energy necessary to develop quality questions. Daniel Willingham, author of *Why Don't Students Like School?* sums it up well, "Sometimes I think that we, as teachers, are so eager to get answers that we do not devote sufficient time to developing the question."

Focus on Questioning, not Quizzing

Here is the essential difference between quizzing and questioning—purpose. The two practices are often thought to be interchangeable but are actually very different. Quizzing involves seeking a short, fact-based, right or wrong answer from a student. They most often contain closed questions that seek to ascertain a specific, correct response. The purpose of a quiz, verbal or written, is to gauge if students have correct knowledge. Questioning, on the other hand, has an expanded purpose and is more aligned with developing the skills called for in the Common Core. The purpose of a question is to uncover understanding. A true question seeks to expose and discover the knowledge, thinking process, or misconceptions of the student. While a quiz

---

Quizzing

Teacher: What is a nocturnal animal?

Student: An animal that stays awake at night.

Teacher: Good. Can you name a nocturnal animal?

Student: Bat.

Questioning

Teacher: What is a nocturnal animal?

Student: An animal that stays awake at night.

Teacher: Tell me more about that. Does a nocturnal animal have any special characteristics?

Student: Well, it doesn't sleep a lot.

Figure 4.1 Quizzing Vs. Questioning

serves the purpose of testing accurate knowledge of a student, a question seeks to understand how that knowledge was developed or how it might be expanded. When a quiz is initiated, the teacher already knows the answer; when a question is asked, the teacher doesn't.

Although we should spend more time questioning and less time quizzing, because it helps to build Common Core skills, it is helpful to remember that the two strategies actually complement each other. As educators, it may be tempting to assume that quizzing will uncover knowledge and help students to expand on their ideas, but only true questions that seek to dig deeper into student understanding will develop the depth necessary for student success. The example in Figure 4.1, developed by Douglas Fisher and Nancy Frey (2007), highlights the essential difference in the outcome between a quiz and a question.

In the example, Fisher and Frey would point out that only through questioning can a teacher truly uncover any misconceptions. As educators, we should develop the habit of consistently asking students to provide evidence, support, or rationale for their ideas or beliefs. Not only does this practice help us to uncover true student understanding, it also helps to place students in the habit of communicating their knowledge—a needed and essential skill of the Common Core.

Beware of the Curse of Knowledge

In the early 1990s, a PhD candidate named Elizabeth Newton described a phenomenon that would later be described as the "curse of knowledge". Newton paired study participants and asked one person to tap out commonly known tunes using their fingers. The second person was tasked with identifying the tune based on the first person's tapping. Newton's experiments showed that the "tappers" and the "listeners" had a difficult time communicating. Listeners got the right tune about 3% of the time. Newton reported that the tappers were often frustrated that their partners couldn't identify the tune. What seemed obvious to the tapper wasn't so obvious to the listener.

This "curse of knowledge" highlights a problem for all educators: once you know something, it is difficult to imagine not knowing it. The tappers had full knowledge of the tune as it was playing in their mind, but their partners only heard random finger tapping. Likewise, when we know something deeply, when we've literally spent thousands of hours thinking about and teaching a concept, it can be a challenge to communicate with those who don't know the concept as deeply.

In their hugely popular book, *Made to Stick* (2008), authors Chip and Dan Heath use the idea of a curse of knowledge to describe why some ideas fail to be memorable. They point out that, "Once you know something, it's hard to imagine not knowing it. And that, in turn, makes it harder for you to communicate to a novice." Research from neuroscience also provides insight into the disconnect between experts and novices. Using brain imaging technology, researchers have studied reaction times and brain processes of amateur and expert chess players. The findings support what Newton found in her research—those who know something deeply (like the expert chess players and teachers) think differently about the content than do amateurs (*National Research Council*, 2000).

So, what does the *curse of knowledge* have to do with questioning? How do we overcome this curse in order to meet the needs of our students? First, do your best to remember what it was like when you first learned the concept you are attempting to teach. As teachers, we are experts in our content. Many of us have literally spent thousands of hours teaching certain concepts and ideas. It is important to remember that while you may have taught a subject hundreds of times, it may be the first time a student has been exposed to those ideas. In many ways we are cursed with the *depth* of knowledge that may make it a challenge to communicate with students. The ideas that are easy for us to understand may in fact be difficult for our students. Therefore, we need to ask probing questions to seek student understanding. If we only quiz students without ever seeking understanding, it can be easy for us to assume that students know the content deeply enough to practice and apply it on the level necessary in the Common Core.

Use Specific Questioning Strategies

If our students are to think deeply and respond thoughtfully to questions and prompts, we need to spend time not only pre-planning which questions we'll ask but also which specific questioning strategies we'll utilize during our lessons. The following strategies have been selected because of their ease of implementation, their universal appeal, and their applicability in all content areas.

Open vs. Closed Questions

A closed question is one that seeks to assess a correct answer. Much like quizzing, closed questions typically ask for a short, right answer that consists of only a few words. A student can usually answer a closed question with a brief answer requiring no elaboration or explanation. A closed question is used when a teacher needs to gauge if a student has some basic knowledge on a topic. Because of the nature of the student responses (brief, only a few words), closed questions almost always involve lower-level responses that rely on memory rather than thoughtful reflection and insight.

An open question is one that seeks to dig deeper to uncover understanding; it is "open" to many possibilities and many answers. When a teacher asks an open question, they are not seeking a pre-determined, correct answer. Rather, they are searching for student understanding and ideas. Open questions require more than a brief interaction between teacher and student; it requires that the teacher solicit responses from students that are unscripted and require thoughtfulness.

Just as quizzing and questioning complement each other, so can open and closed questions be used together to encourage deep thought and reflection. Figure 4.2 outlines some of the characteristic differences between open and closed questions and can serve as a planning tool when developing lessons.

Open Questions	Closed Questions
Require more time	Require less time
Longer responses expected	Shorter responses expected
Require elaboration or explanation	Don't require elaboration or explanation
No correct answer	Correct answer
Benefit from the use of Wait Time/ Think Time	Benefit from the use of Wait Time/ Think Time
Examples:	Examples:
"What are some ways to . . .?"	"What is the name of . . .?"
"How might this result have been different if . . .?"	"Where did _____ take place?"
"What strategies might be best to . . .?"	"What is the answer to _____?"

Figure 4.2 Open Questions Vs. Closed Questions

Focal Points

A problem with many classroom conversations is that students are asked to talk about topics or ideas primarily from memory. That is, they are asked to summarize, talk, or share based on what they remember about the content. Relying primarily in student memory (literally, what is floating around in their minds at any given time) has obvious limitations. Instead, consider providing something for students to look at and study prior to and during their discussion. Focal Points are literally the place where students are to focus their vision and attention during thinking and discussion. Focal Points can be written summaries, an image on a screen, a passage in a book, or a question from a worksheet. This approach sets students up for success because the central focus of the conversation stays the same; the knowledge stays still. Focal Points serve as a reference point to deepen and lengthen discussions and they help to keep students on track and engaged during the interactions.

Question Stems and Sentence Starters

Although Question Stems and Sentence Starters are separate, distinct strategies, they have been combined here because they complement each other so well. A Question Stem is the beginning of a question, typically based on Bloom's Taxonomy that serves as a generic starting point for thinking. Teachers often prepare numerous different Question Stems reflecting the different levels of thinking desired from students. The key to effectively designing and

	Question Stems	Sentence Starters
Used by	Teachers	Students
Developed by	Teachers based on the level of thinking desired by students	Teachers based on the level of thinking desired by students
Based on	Bloom's Taxonomy or a specific cognitive level related to the objective	The desired outcome as determined by the teacher
Examples	"What is the definition of . . .?"	"The best definition for ____ is . . ."
	"What would happen if . . .?"	"If we ____, we would find . . ."
	"What would you ask about . . .?"	"A good question about ____ is . . ."
	"What would a different solution be for . . .?"	"A different solution could be . . ."
	"In your opinion, how would _____ be different if . . .?"	"In my opinion, ____ would be different if . . ."

Figure 4.3 Question Stems and Sentence Starters

using Question Stems is to first determine the type and depth of thinking that will be required of students because the specific verbs used will elicit different thinking and different responses. Sentence Starters, on the other hand, are the specific words and phrases students are to use when responding to questions. They are effective because they allow teachers to direct student thinking towards the specific kinds of responses that will align with the objectives of the lesson. Sentence Starters are also effective for English language learners and for students who struggle to put thoughts or ideas into words. When used in combination, Question Stems and Sentence Starters help to focus student thinking, conversations, and learning. Figure 4.3 contrasts the two strategies and provides some examples of each.

Wait Time/Think Time

Few instructional strategies are as ubiquitous or as well researched as Wait Time. Ever since Mary Budd Rowe conducted her original research in the early 1970s, the concept of Wait Time has become a mainstay in classrooms. In her original studies, she found that teachers on average waited about 1 second after asking question. However, when teachers regularly practiced waiting between 3–5 seconds, the number of students who responded, as well as the quality of those responses increased dramatically. Quite simply, when teachers provide time for students to think about their response, wonderful things happen.

Following up on the research began by Rowe, Robert Stahl described the concept of Think Time and expanded the research to include waiting and pausing at different times during instruction, not just after asking a question. The concept of Think Time, from Stahl's perspective was preferred because, "It names the primary academic purpose and activity of this period of silence—to allow students and the teacher to complete on-task thinking" (Stahl, 1994). In terms of supporting the development of Common Core skills, Wait Time and Think Time, while not new concepts, become as important as ever. As we've discussed throughout the book, students need to develop real-life, transferable skills in addition to mastering content knowledge. Wait Time and Think Time are essential in helping students develop the thinking patterns and habits that will get them to be college and career ready.

Wait Time and Think Time are valuable and effective because they provide opportunities for students to consider their responses to different prompts. When I discuss these ideas with teachers, there is almost a universal acceptance of their usefulness. "So," I often ask, "What is stopping you for more consistently pausing, waiting, and providing time for your students to think?" While the responses are as individual as the teacher, I have assembled common obstacles teachers face when attempting to wait and pause. The list in Figure 4.4 can serve as a tool for self-reflection and discussion.

Since the value and effectiveness of Wait Time/Think Time is well-established, as teachers we should refine and expand our use of this technique so that our students are provided the opportunities to think deeply about topics and concepts. As with any strategy, there are challenges with Wait Time/Think Time. Below are some commonly-asked questions and situations that teachers face with Wait Time/Think Time.

Can I ever provide too much wait time?
Yes, it is possible to pause for too long. Remember that the purpose of pausing is to elicit and promote student thinking. If it becomes apparent that the students are stuck, that they are thinking about things incorrectly, or are overly frustrated, it is best to step back, re-explain, reteach, or move on to another questioning strategy. Recall from Chapter 1 that it is important for students to struggle, but that struggle has to have a purpose. If it becomes clear that the pause is not being productive, move on to another strategy.

What is stopping you from more consistently providing Wait Time or Think Time?

- I don't have enough time.
- We have too much material to cover.
- I'm not in the habit.
- I don't think about it.
- I need to maintain control of the class. If I wait or use silence, off-task behavior could occur.
- I avoid it because I don't know what students are going to say.
- I don't want to embarrass students.
- I don't believe all my students are capable of deep insights or thoughtful answers.
- I don't want students to struggle.
- I'm not comfortable with silence.
- I'm fearful that some student(s) will fill the silence with inappropriate comments.
- I don't really value student input or ideas.
- I have a few students will dominate all discussions.
- I don't know what they are thinking about during the silence. I can't measure it.

Figure 4.4 Reflecting on Obstacles You Face When Implementing Wait or Think Time

When I pause or wait, inevitably some student will blurt something out.
In many classrooms, silence is not the norm. With the exception of testing situations, some students expect that there is some sort of noise or conversation at all times. When there is silence, it can create a level of discomfort that some students are ill-equipped to handle. If you often face this situation, consider utilizing Descriptive Wait Time. This strategy involves literally narrating and describing the process, time, purpose, and outcome of the pause. Some students, surprised by teacher silence (because it may be a rarity), fill the quiet space with comments or questions. Instead of allowing students to fill that void, the teacher makes a pre-emptive statement something to the effect of, "Students, in just a moment I am going to pause and remain silent for about 5 seconds. During this silent time, I want you to consider how you would respond a question I am going to ask." Depending on the needs of the class, the description, or narration may include more details or reminders.

It also may be helpful to ask students to concentrate on a Focal Point or to place a finger over their lips while adopting an "I'm thinking about it" stance.

Sometimes I just forget to pause and wait.
In the middle of a lesson, we can easily become wrapped up in the ideas, the discussions, and the activities to the point where we honestly forget to provide Wait Time/Think Time. If you find yourself in this situation, consider posting a reminder near the clock or in a place where you will see it often during instruction. The reminder can be a picture of a clock with the word wait printed next to it or it can simply be a hand-written note. Another way to remember to wait is to teach students the purpose, value, and how frequently you will be pausing during instruction. Help students learn to be comfortable with silence; help them to understand that silence is not just acceptable, it is absolutely essential to learning.

My calendar is so full of objectives, tasks, and assessments that I don't have time for Wait Time/Think Time. It feels like wasted time.
Every moment in the classroom counts and in the rush to cover everything we have to cover, there can be tendency to fill every second of every class period. However, we have to step back and remember that our job is not to "cover" content; it is to ensure that students learn the content. If student learning is our primary focus, we need to employ strategies that are going to get us to that result. The Common Core Standards challenge the assumption that coverage is a good thing. They call for us to provide opportunities for students to make deep connections among topics and ideas. Pausing, waiting, and providing time for students to think is absolutely necessary if our students are to meet the expectations of the Common Core.

Partner Quiz
Quizzes, when used as an engagement strategy instead of as an assessment tool, can be very effective at focusing student attention on the topics to be addressed during a lesson. Not to be confused with the practice of Quizzing (as in Focus on Questioning, not Quizzing), a Partner Quiz utilizes the power of prediction to engage students. Typically used at the beginning of a lesson, students pair up with partners or small groups to answer a series of questions or comment on a series of statements that relate to the topic that will be addressed during the lesson. True/False questions or Did You Know

type statements serve this purpose very well. For example, to introduce a basic lesson on the brain, students could be asked to share with partners their predictions on the following statements:

True or False? The brain weighs about 10 pounds.

True or False? The brain is hard like the shell of an egg.

True or False? The brain produces enough electricity to power a small light bulb.

When students make predictions and share them verbally with someone else, it produces a desire to know if their predictions are right or not. That internal desire, that need to know if I was correct or not, serves as an effective engagement tool and opens up many opportunities for students to ask and answer questions about the content.

Planted Questions

This strategy encourages participation by offering students the opportunity to consider their thoughts, answers, and ideas to questions *long* before they are asked by the teacher. Planted Questions are typically employed with only a few students at a time and are rarely used as a whole-group strategy. Prior to a lesson, talk privately with the select student(s) and tell them that you have created an easy way for them to participate in class or group discussions. Tell the student(s) the topic of the lesson and then give them a list of a few questions that will be asked during the lesson or small group activity. Ask the student to indicate which question(s) they'd like to answer and provide any clarification if needed. This strategy works effectively for shy, reluctant, or quiet students who rarely volunteer to participate in class discussions. In essence, Planted Questions provide extended Think Time with the added bonus of knowing which question(s) will be asked. It allows for students to consider, over an extended period of time, a response or answer to a question. An extension of this strategy is to also provide students with possible terms or actual answers (called Planted Questions/Planted Answers) to be used in their response. For example, the teacher might say, "Olivia, during the lesson we'll do later today on tectonic plates, I will be asking this question. Here, I've written the question on a 3x5 card for you. I want you to think about how you could respond to that question. When you hear me ask the question, raise your hand and I'll call on you for a response. By the way,

I've included some possible vocabulary words on the back of the card that you could use in your response if you'd like."

Envelope Questions

When students are asked to share ideas with partners or small groups, there are times when interpersonal dynamics make the group ineffective. Sometimes students don't know how to share, sometimes one student dominates a discussion, and sometimes the role of each student is unclear. This strategy offers students a clear method for exchanging ideas and answering questions. Prior to a lesson, brainstorm and list questions that will be asked of students during the lesson. Include a variety of questions at several Bloom's levels as well as open questions that foster discussion. Write each of those questions on a 3x5 card or on a strip of paper and place them in envelopes. Each envelope could have the same questions or the questions could be differentiated based on the needs of the group or pair that will be reading them. Instruct students that they will take turns pulling cards out of the envelope one at a time. After a student pulls a card or strip out of the envelope, they answer the question. The student then places the card/strip to the side and the next partner takes a turn pulling a new question out of the envelope. This process continues until all the questions have been answered.

Q and A Match

This strategy encourages student-to-student exchange of ideas and provides the teacher with a quick and easy method to assess student understanding. After giving each student a set of 3x5 cards or Post-it Notes, provide them with time to review their materials, notes, or books with the purpose of creating questions about the content. Instruct students to write questions on one card or Post-it Note and the corresponding answers on another card or Post-it Note. Provide students with time to research and create their questions and answers. This step is typically done by individual students but it would be permissible to allow pairs of students to create the questions and answers collaboratively. Instruct pairs or small groups to collect all the cards (those with the questions as well as those with the answers) and to shuffle them. On a table, desk, or floor have the students lay all the cards out with the question or answer side showing. Lead students to match the question cards with the corresponding answer card. The students should work collaboratively to match all the cards.

Question/Clarify/Question

This strategy, popularized by Dr Rich Allen, provides a framework and reminder that when asking questions, students often need points of clarification to focus their thinking. This model calls for the teacher to ask a question (typically an open one) followed by information, details, or considerations that help to focus student thinking. This clarification step serves as a way to more clearly state what types of responses the teacher is seeking. Finally, the teacher repeats the original question (adding Wait Time/Think Time) and then prompts students to respond to the question. For example, the teacher might say, "Students, I want you to think about the different tools we could use to display the data we have collected during our surveys. Which of the methods we've learned about in class would be the most useful to graph our results? Would a pie chart, bar graph, or line graph be best? I'll ask you to give a reason for your choice. So, which of the methods we've learned about in class would be the most useful to graph our results?" The power of this approach is that it helps to focus student thinking in a direction that aligns with the objective of the lesson. The clarification step is also valuable for students who may get sidetracked or off-track in their thinking because it provides examples or details the student might not have thought of on their own.

Objectives into Questions

A simple, but extremely effective way to incorporate more questions into instruction is to take statements, objectives, and other "facts" and turn them into questions. It is quite common for teachers to write objectives on the board for students to refer to during a lesson. Many teachers are even in the practice of posting student-friendly objectives in order to help build comprehension and relevance among students. However, let's be honest, objectives are for teachers. They are tools teachers use to focus the academic activities towards the desired outcome. Students typically care little about objectives. They care more about the activities, the interaction, and the things they get to do during the lesson. Because students care about what they get to do, consider turning objectives into questions and then aligning those questions to the activities of the lesson. I am not suggesting that teachers stop creating objectives. On the contrary, objectives are necessary and important. However, when communicating objectives to students, questions can be an effective tool for engaging them in the learning.

Summary

When teachers employ effective questioning strategies it increases the likelihood that students will engage in the life of the classroom and develop the skills referenced throughout the Common Core Standards. When students think about questions, respond to questions from others, and ask their own questions, they are developing essential life-long skills that will enable them to be college and career ready.

Reflection Questions

1. On a scale of 1–10, how would you rate your current questioning skills? How would you rate the current level of your students in their ability to respond to questions? Is there a gap between your skills and your students' abilities? What might account for any differences?

2. Of the teachers you remember growing up, which ones had exceptional questioning skills? What were some of their characteristics or practices that you remember most?

3. Imagine you are talking with someone who had little knowledge of effective questioning practices. How would you explain the difference between quizzing and questioning?

4. The concept of a Curse of Knowledge has been used to describe the gap between an expert and a novice. In your teaching, in what areas are you *cursed* by a depth of knowledge that may make it a challenge to communicate with students?

5. Of the specific questioning strategies outlined in the chapter, which ones are the most applicable for your setting? How might you adjust any of the strategies to best meet the needs of your students?

Extend Your Knowledge

- In the book *Classroom Instruction that Works* by Robert Marzano, Debra Pickering, and Jane Pollock, the authors differentiate between cues and questions. Although they serve a similar function, they are not the same. A cue is a "hint" that a teacher provides to guide the student towards the information, process, or evidence that they'll use during a learning task. A question seeks an answer while a cue does not.

- Barbara Blackburn's book *Rigor is NOT a Four-Letter Word* outlines nine elements of good questions and does an excellent job connecting the questioning to rigor.

- Socratic Seminars are often referenced when discussing questioning and its relation to learning. Read *Teaching in the Block—Strategies for Engaging Active Learners,* by Robert Lynn Canady and Michael Rettig, for a great overview of the benefits, challenges, and the distinctions between a Socratic Seminar and a classroom discussion.

- The book *Quality Questioning* by Jackie Walsh and Beth Sattes provides a helpful overview of the research base that supports the use of questioning in the classroom. Included are helps and tips that assist teachers when developing questions.

- Most people know of Benjamin Bloom because of the taxonomy of educational objectives he helped create. Although he is best known for Bloom's Taxonomy, he had a career that spanned five decades of research that included a look at topics ranging from early childhood education to assessment. For a great overview of the life of this amazing educator, read *Benjamin Bloom—Portraits of an Educator* edited by Thomas Guskey.

Critical Thinking in the Common Core Classroom

Key Idea

If students are to exhibit the skills of the Common Core, they need to think critically about their knowledge, about their understanding, and about their own skills and abilities. Critical thinking is a commonly-cited 21st-Century skill that students must possess and regularly utilize if they are going to be college and career ready.

What Is Critical Thinking?

Consider for a moment how you would respond to the following statements related to critical thinking. Do you agree or disagree with these statements?

Schools often unknowingly discourage critical thinking.

Complaining is a form of critical thinking.

In many classrooms, compliant behavior is more important than individual thought.

The more we get students to think critically, the better they'll become at it.

Critical thinking is a skill that must be taught and a habit that must be practiced.

Students don't like to think critically.

Students intrinsically trust the written word. They automatically assume that what they read is correct.

The ability to think critically is often cited as a shortcoming of high school graduates as they enter college. Studies that follow college graduates also cite a lack of problem-solving, interpersonal, and analytical skills as they enter the workforce (Arum & Roksa, 2010). Employers often complain that graduates don't have the ability to resolve conflicts and that they lack the thinking and logic skills necessary to perform their jobs effectively. In 2013, *Forbes Magazine* cross-referenced the ten most in-demand skills that are required in the ten most in-demand jobs. That is, they looked beyond knowledge of programs, content, or technical training to the actual skills that job candidates must possess in order to thrive in their careers. They found the following skills, listed in order, in the descriptions of nine of the ten most in-demand jobs: 1. Critical Thinking; 2. Complex Problem Solving; 3. Judgment and Decision-Making; 4. Active Listening.

Although graduates often possess content knowledge in disciplines such as math or science, they often lack the interpersonal, communication, and critical thinking skills necessary to truly thrive in the workplace. Needless to say, this is a topic that requires significant attention from educators. Building critical thinking skills and habits in students is something that needs to begin at the very youngest grades. Students literally need years of practice, starting in elementary school and continuing through their entire schooling experience, in order to be prepared to be college and career ready.

What then, is critical thinking? A review of the academic research will result in a dizzying array of definitions, comparisons, and analogies. Fields of study varying from education to business to neuroscience have weighed in on the topic and have offered their unique perspectives. Regardless of the varying backgrounds and approaches different disciplines take when discussing critical thinking, there are some commonalities and concepts that rise to the surface that are helpful for educators to consider.

It is helpful to think of critical thinking as a skill that needs to be developed and practiced over time in order for it to become a habit. The more any of us practice a skill, the better we become at it. For those educators who get frustrated that students don't seem to want to think critically, consider how often students are truly given the opportunity to develop and practice the skill. Could it be that our students do truly want to think critically, but they are just not in the habit of it? Consider also that critical thinking can take many different forms, including complaining, criticizing, and disapproving.

Daniel Willingham, author of *Why Don't Students Like School?* points out that while the brain isn't particularly good at critical thinking (it's slow, unreliable, and effortful, he says), we actually like to do it. We like puzzles, scenarios, conundrums, and problems. When we are appropriately challenged, critical thinking can be fun and intrinsically motivating. After all, who doesn't like to solve other people's problems?

Schools and classrooms also sometimes unknowingly discourage critical thinking. Most classrooms are designed for stability, routine, and predictability. Students certainly need a level of predictability for emotional security and a sense of belonging in the classroom but in the process of creating safe, predictable, and secure environments we sometimes focus more on compliant behavior than we do on critical thought. While we need compliant student behavior in order to have a well-run classroom, we may unwittingly (or overtly in some cases) be sending the message that divergent thinking isn't valued.

Consider what we most often reward in classrooms; we reward those students who do what they are told. Grades, character celebrations, extrinsic rewards, positive notes homes, etc. almost always go to the kids who have figured out the system—*do what you're told, hand in work on time, be polite, and don't challenge the teacher.* The recipe for success in most schools and classrooms is compliant behavior. As educators, we may need to realize that pure compliance and deep critical thought may sometimes be in conflict. While we say we want students to think critically, most classrooms don't reward thinking as much a student's ability to follow directions and remain silent when they are supposed to.

Of all the definitions, concepts, and approaches to critical thinking, my favorite quote comes from Ben Johnson, author of *Teaching Students to Dig Deeper.* He says, "critical thinking is all about doubting what you read, hear, or see and asking the hard questions, the politically-charged questions, and the socially inconvenient questions." His definition reminds us of our responsibility to our students as well as our responsibility to ourselves and to the greater profession. The ultimate goal of asking the questions and doubting what you learn is decision making. After all, the goal and purpose of critical thinking and education in general is to make a decision. Critical thinking is not the end but a means to the end. Our students need to be critical thinkers and problem solvers so that they can make appropriate decisions, communicate effectively, and use proof to support conclusions.

Critical Thinking in the Common Core

Regardless of who is to blame for students' lack of critical thinking skills, it is clear that our students need to develop this skill in order to meet the expectations of the Common Core. Because the term *critical thinking* does not appear in the national version of the Common Core Standards, it might be helpful to view it as a generic term for a foundational skill set upon which other more discreet skills are built. For example, in order for students to persuade, argue, reason, describe, persevere, or critique they need to undertake varying degrees of critical thinking. In other words, those things don't happen without a baseline ability to think critically.

In addition, critical thinking is central to much of what we've discussed in previous chapters. In order for students to persevere through struggle and error (Chapter 1), they need to think critically about their progress, their own internal thinking processes, and reflect on their successes. In order for students to build self-regulation skills (Chapter 2), they need to regularly reflect on their own development and how their behavior supports their growth. Rigorous learning (Chapter 3) is about the depth, complexity, and personal connections students make with the content. Application of deep, rigorous learning cannot take place without critical thinking. Questioning (Chapter 4) is, at its core, about seeking understanding. Well-developed and well-delivered questions get kids to think deeply and critically. Finally, in Chapter 6 we'll address the importance of getting students to engage in academically-focused conversations. In order to engage in the type of conversation and dialogue called for in the Common Core, students will need to be able think critically about their own ideas and the ideas of others.

Strategies to Promote Critical Thinking

Early on in my career a colleague shared the following quote with me and it has stuck with me ever since. "A good teacher is one who puts you in a situation where you have to think to get out." Although I've never been able to confirm the author of the saying, I've always imagined it came from some wise educator who had unlocked the secrets to getting students to think deeply. The truth is that there are no secrets and there is no singular, correct way to get students to think critically. Rather, there are countless

In order for students to be successful with critical thinking, you should incorporate the following items into your planning and teaching.

- *Preplan the activities*—If I want my students to think critically, I have to plan for it. Consequently, I need to have an intimate knowledge of the skills and abilities of all my students because not all students can, or should be expected to, undertake the same critical thinking tasks.

- *Integrate critical thinking*—Critical thinking should be viewed as a skill that is integrated into and with the content being learned. It shouldn't be viewed as something else that needs to be done, but rather as a natural extension of comprehension and knowledge. Students will be much more likely to experience success when critical thinking instruction is integrated within a discipline rather than when it is taught as a stand-alone topic.

- *Tell students the what, why, and how*—Students need to know the purpose, rationale, and relevance of the thinking tasks in addition to procedures for resources, outcomes, time limits, and people to work with. Remember that critical thinking is a developed, learned skill and that students need overt instruction in the how, why, and what needs to be done to achieve the goal.

- *Ensure progress is being made by all students*—Remember that students will actually enjoy critical thinking given the right conditions. With the right support, guidance, feedback, and instruction, they can learn to think critically. However, it is extremely important to remember that each, individual student must experience some level of success and progress during the learning task. Motivation will likely wither if students put forth the effort to think critically but don't experience any movement towards the goal.

Figure 5.1 Teacher's Checklist to Ensure Student Success with Critical Thinking

methods and strategies that may work, given the right conditions. Figure 5.1 is a checklist that will help you ensure students are thinking critically.

With that checklist in mind, the following strategies are offered because of their ease of use, their effectiveness, and their applicability in many content areas and in a variety of grade levels.

Writing

In relation to the development of critical thinking skills, writing is perhaps the most versatile and effective strategy teachers have at their disposal. In the context of teaching critical thinking skills, a focus on writing-to-learn (instead of learning to write) is important because the act of writing *is the act of thinking*. Consider it this way; we have all at times sat down to compose an email, a note, or a narrative without knowing exactly what we wanted to say or how to say it. The process of writing helped us to clarify our thoughts and ideas. We are typically clearer in our beliefs or thoughts after we have undertaken a writing task. That is, when a person writes, they must utilize thinking, planning, and reflective processes to create a piece of writing that meets its intended goal. When one undertakes a writing task they must take internal thoughts, ideas, perceptions, questions, and knowledge and translate them into words on paper that are coherent and communicate effectively. Furthermore, writing-to-learn can increase engagement, improve memory, deepen understanding, provide a source for feedback, serve as a reference point during discussions, and help students to find meaning in content.

Since critical thinking is expected for all levels of students, writing-to-learn is a strategy that should be incorporated in all content areas, at all grades, and at many times during the day. Writing can include lists, quick writes, summaries, essays, narratives, formal and informal letters, emails, reports, journals, notes, dialogue, and free writing to name a few. The point here is that writing-to-learn is not synonymous with an essay that gets evaluated and graded. In fact, the Common Core places a greater emphasis on argumentation in writing (providing proof or evidence to support a conclusion) and informational writing than it does on narrative writing.

When assigning writing tasks, it is important for teachers to overtly teach the characteristics of the type of effective writing that is expected. That is, we need to teach writing, not merely assign writing. For example, if students are asked to self-reflect in a journal entry they need to be taught the process and characteristics of an effective journal entry. Merely telling students to write more will not get them to develop and practice the critical thinking skills they need. The website www.teachingthecore.com summarizes well the power of thinking through writing, "The point is as simple as it is profound: if you've got students writing all the time for a lot of stuff, you're nailing W.CCR.10 and, infinitely more important, you're giving kids the reading/writing version of the mutant spider that bites Peter Parker."

"Says Who?"

This strategy is effective because of its simplicity, power, and direct connection to critical thinking. When a student responds to a question, offers an opinion, or gives an explanation the teacher should regularly respond with, "Says who?" This practice serves as a good reminder to probe for understanding (which is the nature of true questioning as discussed in Chapter 4) in order to accurately gauge student knowledge or skills. The Common Core standards place an emphasis, in both ELA and Math, on providing proof and evidence for statements and conclusions. Students need to be appropriately challenged and asked to regularly provide such evidence. In addition, this strategy supports the need for students to analyze the information they are reading, accessing, or using to construct arguments.

When utilizing the "Says Who?" strategy, it is important to note that the manner in which the question is asked is important. "Says Who?" should not come across as an accusation or said in a manner in which the teacher doubts the student (and certainly not with any sarcastic tone). Rather, tell students that the goal of the question is to make sure they have some evidence to support their ideas.

The "Says Who?" question should also be adjusted to meet the context of the discussion and the objective of the learning. For example, variations of the question could be "Convince me", "Why?", "Prove it", or "What makes you think that?" As with all questioning strategies, utilize Think Time and follow up with probing questions that force students to dig a little deeper into their thinking.

Agree/Disagree Statements

Few things motivate students to participate and think as much as the ability to agree or disagree with the teacher and/or with each other. This strategy allows students to express an opinion, consider the ideas and opinions of others, and discuss important ideas. Agree/Disagree Statements support critical thinking because they force students to make a choice. That is, when statements are well-designed in order to elicit deeper thinking, students must defend their position or opinion. Refer back to the beginning of this chapter. I provided several Agree/Disagree statements related to the topic of critical thinking that were designed to consider the topic from various points of view.

Prior to a lesson, choose three or more statements that can be made about the content. After getting students' attention, instruct them that they'll need to signal agreement or disagreement with the statements that will be made. Signaling can take the form of standing, thumbs up, walking to a corner, or holding up an Agree/Disagree card. Make statements one at a time and ask students to signal a response to each statement. After students have signaled their agree or disagree stance, provide an opportunity for them to discuss their stance both with those who agree as well as with those who disagree. When students are discussing their opinions, consider asking Open Questions or using the "Says Who?" strategy to elicit deeper thinking.

Envelope Sorts

Sorting, as a strategy to encourage thinking and divergent thought, is a powerful and simple tool to help students to practice the skill of critical thinking. When students sort items, vocabulary words, concepts, pictures, or objects there is a need for them to consider the characteristics, definitions, or qualities that items have in common or what characteristics they have that are different. Although sorting can be a simple task when the rules and guidelines are simple and explained, sorting can actually be a very complex process. A simple task, for example, might require students to sort word cards by their beginning sound.

However, a more complex sort might be what educators refer to as an open sort. During an open sort, students are asked to sort items, concepts, or words without being given any direction on how to arrange them. As a collaborative activity, open sorts require students to communicate, consider each other's ideas, create group consensus, negotiate, and finally agree to a set of conclusions. For example, the following math terms could be placed on 3x5 cards and placed in an envelope: quadrilateral, parallelogram, rhombus, square, rectangle, and trapezoid. A closed sort might involve students sorting those terms according to specific definitions or examples. An open sort might involve the teacher saying something to the effect of, "Students, in the envelopes on your table are 3x5 cards with math terms on them. With your partners, your job is to sort or categorize those terms in any way that makes sense to the group. You should talk with your partners about how and why you are sorting them in a particular way. Be ready to provide reasons for your decisions."

Close Reading

The Common Core calls for students to read and understand increasingly complex texts. In fact, text complexity is a term that is used often in discussions regarding the ELA standards. Close Reading is an approach to help students make sense of and understand complex texts. Not to be confused with Cloze activities, Close Reading is a general term for a set of strategies that encourage students to look closely at the reading tasks in front of them.

Close reading can be contrasted with the idea of surface reading; a process where a reader does not pay close attention to details, information, or context of a passage. Douglas Fisher, author of numerous books including *Teaching Students to Read Like Detectives,* says that Close Reading involves careful and purposeful re-reading of a text (Fisher, Frey, & Lapp, 2011, 107). He states that students should examine and analyze a text with the purpose of "unpacking" the meaning. Close Reading serves several purposes as it relates to Common Core skills: it leads to deeper understanding, it facilitates discussion, it builds habits, and it increases vocabulary. Although there is not one singular strategy or definition of Close Reading, the following quote from Timothy Shanahan provides some food for thought.

> Close reading requires a substantial emphasis on readers figuring out a high quality text. This "figuring out" is accomplished primarily by reading and discussing the text (as opposed to being told about the text by a teacher or being informed about it through some textbook commentary). Because challenging texts do not give up their meanings easily, it is essential that readers re-read such texts (not all texts are worth close reading).

Close Reading, as a strategy to build critical thinking, involves multiple, purposeful readings of the same text. The first reading of a text is typically done in order for students to build comprehension. After a first reading, students should be able to answer basic questions about the content, ideas, or concepts from the reading. Depending on the ability level of the students, it is often recommended that students complete this first reading on their own. After students have a basic understanding of the content of the text, a second reading requires that they go deeper into the text in order to consider data, evidence, literary elements, organization of the text, choice of vocabulary, etc. This second reading is about figuring out what the text said, not just what it was about. A third reading, then, is about going even deeper into the text in order to discover meaning and to make personal connections. Depending on the needs of the students, second and third readings do not have to include the entire text nor do they have to be the same for all students.

Use this checklist to design effective close reading lessons.

- Select a short, robust passage for students to read (a scene from a play, a passage from a book, a poem, a letter, etc.).
- Plan ahead in order to identify the vocabulary to teach, the questions to ask, and to identify areas of the text that may provide challenges to students.
- Have students read the passage on their own initially. Instruct students to annotate or question as they read. Do not read the text to students nor provide them with definitions or context until after the first read, if possible.
- Prompt students to process the text. This can be done via a quick write or a discussion.
- Model read the passage for students focusing on prosody (expression and fluency) and/or thinking aloud about elements of the passage that relate to evidence, data, literary devices, etc.
- Lead students to do a third read asking them to note what they missed the first time. Ask students to focus on the author's meaning and connections to their own life.
- Ask text-dependent questions that require knowledge gained from the reading.

Figure 5.2 Checklist for Creating Close Reading Activities

Shanahan summarizes the three readings this way, "Thus, close reading is an intensive analysis of a text in order to come to terms with what it says, how it says it, and what it means."

The checklist in Figure 5.2 can serve as a helpful guideline when creating activities in which students need to read closely.

Summary

In order for students to be college and career ready, they need to have the ability to employ critical thinking skills strategically in order to make decisions and to reach goals. Critical thinking is a learned skill and, as such, needs to be taught and practiced over time if students are to truly develop a habit of thinking. Burris and Garrity (2012) remind us that, "Engaging students in critical thinking . . . is not only motivational, it is the best way that we can prepare our students for postsecondary education and for the 21st century workplace."

Reflection Questions

1. At the beginning of the chapter, there were seven agree/disagree statements listed. How might you use this strategy with your students? What variations or extensions could you incorporate in order to get your students to think critically?

2. If you don't totally agree that most classrooms reward compliant behavior more than critical thinking, consider the nature of the comments listed on student report cards. Do more of the comments focus on behavior ("The student is respectful and a good member of his/her team") or academic skills such as critical thinking?

3. Imagine a parent or colleague asked you about critical thinking. What terms or concepts would you use to define it? Could you define critical thinking in just a few words?

4. How might you explain to students the need to think critically as it relates to their success in school and life beyond school? What benefits can you outline to students besides a response that, "You'll need to think critically when you get into college"?

5. Sometimes teachers report that their students don't like to write. They report that students grumble, complain, and sometimes outright refuse to write. Why might this be the case? What is the relationship between the type of writing asked of students and their motivation? What strategies do you employ to get your students to enjoy writing?

Extend Your Knowledge

- *Teaching Students to Dig Deeper—The Common Core in Action* by Ben Johnson is a great resource for ideas and strategies that focus on critical thinking and communication including a great comparison of the pros and cons of critical thinking.

- To read more about the brain processes involved in critical thinking, read chapter 1 of Daniel Willingham's book *Why Don't Students Like School?* In it, Dr Willingham explains that brains typically rely more on memory than critical thinking.

- In order for students to succeed in developing critical thinking skills, they need consistent, positive, and honest feedback about their progress. For a great resource on the topic, read Jane Pollock's book *Feedback: The Hinge that Joins Teaching and Learning.*

- Art Costa and Bean Kallick have been pioneers in the area of thinking skills with their work centered on Habits of Mind. Check out their website at www.instituteforhabitsofmind.com/.

- The checklist on page 65 reminds teachers of the importance of pre-planning activities to engage students in critical thinking. However, not all activities labeled or described as critical thinking actually require students to think critically. When reviewing textbooks or published materials, don't take for granted a statement that an activity or question develops critical thinking. As educators, we need to think critically and question someone's claims that their product develops critical thinking skills.

6 Academic Conversations in the Common Core Classroom

Key Idea

If students are to exhibit the skills of the Common Core, they need to know how to have academically-focused conversations that are in-depth, meaningful, and sustained. The ability to verbalize knowledge and understanding and to interact with a variety of people in the process is necessary if students are to be college and career ready.

What is an Academic Conversation?

Let's be honest, there are few excellent models of polite, effective dialogue in our society. Consider the talk we hear from the media, from politicians, and even in sports and entertainment. The crude, the brash, the violent, and the aggressive get our attention. What we often see is people talking over each other with little desire to truly understand or appreciate differing views and ideas. It's not uncommon to hear shouting, yelling, threats, and name-calling all in an effort to win an argument and persuade others. Is it any wonder, then, that many of our students do not know how to have a respectful, focused, and effective conversation? As long as we are being honest, schools aren't always effective models of discourse either. We often see the same types of disrespectful interactions in the schoolhouse as we do in every other part of society. However, our students deserve better. They deserve better models and better tools to deal with normal conflicts that arise when people interact and share ideas. We have an obligation to teach our students the skills of effective communication.

Traditionally, far too many schools and far too many teachers have treated student talk as unnecessary. In some cases, talk is seen as the enemy of a productive and efficient classroom. For decades we have assumed that the primary role of the learner is to watch and listen. Passive, compliant students are often held up as models with the goal of creating students that are seen and not heard. The predominant theory for years was that students were merely blank slates that needed to be impressed upon. Thus, the best, most efficient way to get students the knowledge they needed was to have them sit and listen. This belief—that students learn best through passive observation with a focus on solo, independent work—still permeates much of the education culture. However, we know that learning is a dynamic, interactive process that requires significant engagement and effort on the part of the learner. While some students do excel and achieve in the kind of environments described above, the suggestion that learning is best achieved for all students through a passive "receiving" of information does not hold up to current research and science (Marzano, 2007).

Jeff Zwiers and Marie Crawford, in their thoughtful book, *Academic Conversations—Classroom Talk that Fosters Critical Thinking and Content Understandings,* define academic conversations as, "sustained and purposeful conversations about school topics". For our purposes here, as it relates to the Common Core, we will define academic conversation as student talk that builds and deepens content knowledge, enhances skill development, and engages students in the life of the classroom. Generally, throughout this chapter the terms *conversation* and *talk* will be used synonymously. While there are clear differences between them, the goal is the same: to get students to engage in talk that centers on the topics, content, and subject matter that will lead to greater understanding and knowledge while in the process helping them to develop the necessary skills to survive in the 21st Century.

Academic Conversations and the Common Core

There is ample evidence from the research that student conversation about academic topics is effective at building content knowledge and engaging students. Yet, despite the power of student talk, it is rare. Teacher talk still dominates most classrooms (Fisher, Frey, & Rothenberg, 2008). If our students are to meet the expectations of the Common Core, things will have to change. To this point, there aren't any other options; students will need to be much more involved in talking about academic topics if they are going to be successful and meet the demands of the Common Core. However, even beyond the requirements of the Common Core, think about the skill set graduates will need to possess if they are going to be competitive in the world economy. As educators, we have a responsibility to help our students achieve standards but we also have a responsibility to prepare them to be successful in life. Helping them build conversational tools will do both.

The English Language Arts Standards have obvious and direct implications for academic talk. Those standards are flush with verbs such as *ask, answer, produce, recount, participate, initiate,* and *respond.* The introduction to the Speaking and Listening Anchor standards (which are imbedded in the ELA Standards) has this to say about the importance of conversation:

> To build a foundation for college and career readiness, students must have ample opportunities to take part in a variety of rich, structured conversations—as part of a whole class, in small groups, and with a partner. Being productive members of these conversations requires that students contribute accurate, relevant information; respond to and develop what others have said; make comparisons and contrasts; and analyze and synthesize a multitude of ideas in various domains.
>
> *www.corestandards.org/ELA-Literacy/CCRA/SL*

This is a tall order; to prepare students with those kinds of skills will take an intentional focus. The Common Core standards make it very clear that teachers at every grade level and in every content area have a role to play in teaching all the standards. The teaching of the kind of skills and behaviors listed above needs to start in the very youngest grades in order to set the foundation for success in future grades.

The importance of academically-focused student talk is clear when looking at the English Language Arts Standards. However, beyond the obvious connections in the ELA Standards, a closer look at the Common Core Math Standards will also reveal the need for students to communicate their knowledge and understanding. The Math Standards include verbs such as *describe, interpret, summarize, evaluate,* and *explain.* While it is still important for students to be able to follow algebraic rules and to have their basic math facts memorized, the Common Core also calls for students to be able to explain and rationalize their knowledge. The Introduction to the Math Standards says this about the importance of helping students to truly understand math:

> One hallmark of mathematical understanding is the ability to justify, in a way appropriate to the student's mathematical maturity, why a particular mathematical statement is true or where a mathematical rule comes from. There is a world of difference between a student who can summon a mnemonic device to expand a product . . . and a student who can explain where the mnemonic comes from.

While an in-depth view of any of the standards is beyond the scope of this chapter, we can start to see a theme throughout the Common Core—active learning, student participation, and engagement in talking about their learning and knowledge is central to helping students meet content standards and 21st-Century skills.

If classrooms are to become more intentional places in relation to teaching Common Core skills such as conversation, norms may have to change. Norms, in this context, refer to the sometimes hidden rules we follow when designing learning opportunities for students. In other words, our norms serve as a guide for how we "do" school. From the very first years in school, it should become the expectation that students talk about what they learn. Conversations, dialogues, and discussions should become *the central feature* of every classroom. Again, while this is no easy task, it is absolutely necessary if students are to be successful in a world in which they will have to exhibit the skills we've highlighted throughout this book.

Promoting Academic Conversations

Linda Darling-Hammond, in her landmark book *The Right to Learn,* points out that, "Talking is a vehicle for learning." She discusses the importance of allowing students the opportunity to articulate what they know through discussions and conversations, thus offering them the chance to externalize their thinking. The process of externalizing thinking through talking is an essential element to personal growth as well as the development of content knowledge. One of the most important things we can do as educators is provide multiple, meaningful ways for students to externalize their thinking through talk, conversation, dialogue, and discussion. So, our big question as it relates to the Common Core is, "How do we increase the likelihood that students will engage in academically-focused conversations?"

Three Building Blocks of Effective Student Conversations

When combined in a thoughtful and intentional way, the three building blocks of curiosity, purpose, and structure have the opportunity to engage students in focused and productive conversations. These elements, when used in unison, promote academic conversations by providing a useful framework for teachers to utilize when designing tasks and activities for students. In other words, curiosity + purpose + structure = an increased likelihood that students will engage in conversations that will refine their skills and develop their content knowledge.

Curiosity

As the first of the three building blocks, the role of curiosity is to ignite thinking on the part of the students. If we want students to talk about their learning, we need spark an internal desire to learn something. Curiosity is all about placing information, situations, context, or problems in front of students that stimulate in them the desire to think. Unfortunately, classrooms are often places where intellectual curiosity takes a back seat to the objectives, facts, and "stuff" students need to master on state-mandated assessments. The first step in getting students to talk about academic topics is to give them something interesting to talk about.

Judy Willis, neuroscientist turned middle school teacher, points out that once curiosity is piqued, our brains will naturally be on the lookout for additional information that can help to shed light on the topic. This state of "disequilibrium-prompted curiosity", as she calls it, is a powerful motivator that helps to engage students in the tasks placed before them (Willis, 2007). John Medina, another well-known neuroscientist and author of the highly-regarded book *Brain Rules,* has declared that curiosity should be the single most important and "vital" feature of school (Medina, 2008). Because curiosity is so important in learning, it provides the perfect starting point for academic discussions.

We greatly increase the chance that students will engage in a discussion if they are curious about a topic. Therefore, when designing lessons and learning opportunities for students, first take a close look at the content that students will be asked to discuss. The subjects and ideas students will be asked to discuss need to be age-appropriate, interesting, relevant to student experiences, and provide the substance necessary to carry on a sustained and focused conversation.

Purpose

While curiosity can spark an interest in a topic, students also need to know the purpose for having a discussion. Curiosity alone will not guarantee that students will engage in a discussion nor will it be sufficient in helping a student make the content-oriented connections that will help them to deepen their knowledge and understanding. In other words, curiosity without purpose is incomplete. Therefore, we need to give consideration to the purpose and rationale we provide to students that outline the reasons for having an academic discussion.

Once we pique student curiosity with interesting information, it should be followed with a clear, compelling purpose for having a discussion. The purpose for classroom discussions should center on the exchange of ideas and the deepening of content knowledge. Because motivation is likely already increased by attending to curiosity, the most simple, straightforward reasons are the best. The purpose could be stated as simply as, "Students, in order for you to think more about this topic, you will be having a conversation with your peers. This conversation will allow you an opportunity to hear what some other people think about this topic."

While it is likely that some students will need a more overt, reward-oriented purpose for participating in a discussion, it is recommended that points, grades, and incentives not become the central focus of the purpose for academic conversations. A spotlight on what students will get (or on what they will not get) has the very real chance of sidetracking conversations away from an authentic purpose. What we want is for students to engage in genuine, focused conversations that deepen their knowledge while at the same time refining their skills as a communicator. An overreliance on extrinsic motivators is not compatible with the development of true, lasting skills because the purpose shifts away from learning towards doing what is necessary to get the points or please the teacher.

Structure

The structure serves as the final building block of effective student conversations. In this context, structure refers to the format, methods, and strategies students will use to participate in a discussion. In essence, the structure constitutes the *rules of the game* for the conversation. Without a specific structure, conversations often fall apart or fail to reach their full potential. It may be most beneficial to think of the structure as the specific strategies that the teacher will use to engage students in conversation. Structure/strategy is listed as the last of the three building blocks because the specific strategy utilized depends upon the content, the purpose, and the needs of the students.

There are probably hundreds of strategies that could be used to promote conversations between students. In addition to ones that have been shared in other chapters, below are five additional simple and easy-to-implement strategies that increase the likelihood that students will engage in academically-focused conversations:

- **Think–Write–Pair–Share**—This strategy, or variations of it, has been in the toolbox of teachers for years. The power of this strategy is that it provides a physical, external source of knowledge and ideas that can help to focus and extend student conversations. After providing students with a relevant topic or question, give them some time to think about a response. Then prompt them to write that response down on paper. The written response then becomes the tangible object students will use when they pair with partners and share ideas.

- **Conversation Extenders**—Much like the strategy of Sentence Starters shared in Chapter 4, Conversation Extenders are sentence stems that are used to extend and deepen a conversation. Students need to understand that there are natural lulls or periods of silence during any conversation. It is easy to assume that when these silent periods arise that the conversation is over. However, conversations can almost always be extended and expanded with the use of questions such as,

    "Did you think about . . ."
    "What would happen if . . ."
    "You said _____. Tell me more about that . . ."
    "The most interesting thing I heard you say was . . ."

- **Flip the Brainstorm**—Traditional brainstorming sessions often rely on the input and ideas of just a few participants. Because classroom brainstorming sessions are typically conducted with the entire class, they become susceptible to interpersonal and group dynamics. As a result, they often fail to garner input and ideas from everyone in the group and they also usually fail to produce individual ownership of the ideas agreed upon. As an alternative, consider a flipped brainstorm. This variation *first* asks students to consider problems, scenarios, or issues on their own. Rather than immediately gathering information from everyone in the group, the first step is getting participants to think about the topic on their own without input from anyone else. This first step is crucial because it provides an opportunity for students to think of their own ideas absent any other influence. Then, once students have brainstormed solutions on their own, they are asked to pair with a partner or small group to explain their ideas. This second step provides a chance for students to refine and clarify their ideas in the safety of a small group. These first two steps increase the commitment and personal involvement in the development of ideas and solutions to the problem presented to the class. The third and final step is then presenting refined ideas to the whole group.

- **Gallery Walk**—This strategy utilizes physical movement and an external Focal Point (see Chapter 4 for a more complete description of Focal Points) in a natural, comfortable way that mirrors what happens in real life. Prior to the lesson create several questions, examples, or images that align to the objective. Post those on the walls around the room and ask students to pair with a partner to walk around the room and discuss the questions or remark on the content. Named after what adults do naturally when visiting a museum or exhibit, students are encouraged to discuss their reactions, thoughts, and ideas.

- **Partner Pretest**—When combined with some of the other strategies such as Think–Write–Pair–Share or Conversation Extenders, a Partner Pretest can serve as a relevant and engaging method for students to talk about their knowledge as they prepare for an assessment. Students know that tests are important and most of them sincerely desire to do well. Place students in partners or small groups and prompt them to discuss topics, questions, or problems that are likely to appear on an upcoming assessment. Students could also rank or describe their confidence in that knowledge and what they might do to better prepare for the assessment.

Managing Academic Conversations

Talking is not the enemy of learning—in fact it is essential to learning. Talkative students are not a problem; they are a necessity. The challenge, of course, is getting students to focus their talk on academic topics and getting them to engage in conversations that deepen their content understanding. An increase in student talk in the classroom will necessitate an increased focus on the methods teachers use to manage that talk. While true, authentic, and meaningful conversations are difficult things to control, there are some guidelines that teachers can use to help manage the process.

Teach Students about the Art of Conversation

Prior to engaging students in the specific structures or strategies, spend time instructing them on the finer points of effective verbal communication. Depending on the age of the students, consider teaching them about the role of listening, the importance of non-verbal communication and body language, and how to take turns. However, regardless of the age of the students, there are some universal things all students should know as it relates to effective discussions. The earlier they learn and internalize these important truths, the better:

- Effective, meaningful conversations can be difficult. Not only can conversations be challenging, they can also be frustrating, exhilarating, confusing, rewarding, and fun. Students need to be aware that they will likely experience a range of emotions during conversations and that those reactions are normal, expected, and healthy.

- They will be required to interact and communicate with people who have a variety of communication abilities. Not everyone they talk with will have the same set of expectations or skills and they need to be able to adjust to the situation in order to effectively exchange ideas. The goal is rarely to have a "winner". Rather, the objective is to exchange ideas, learn from, and appreciate each other.

- Like almost everything else in life, becoming an expert communicator takes practice and persistence. As a skill, effective communication via conversation, discussion, and dialogue will be refined over a period of a lifetime and the goal is to become better with each passing week.

Model, Monitor, and Provide Feedback

Managing what some would describe as the "controlled chaos" of lots of student talk requires coherent models, consistent monitoring of student actions, and immediate feedback about progress. The importance of modeling here cannot be understated. Students need clear examples of what effectiveness looks like and it is rarely sufficient to model just once for students. Rather, provide visual models, images, and role playing opportunities so that students know what to expect with each interaction and conversation. While students are participating in conversations, consistently monitor what is happening in order to provide immediate and constructive feedback about their progress. This process of monitoring and providing feedback is crucial for keeping students focused on the task at hand. Monitoring and feedback is also particularly important for students that may struggle with inappropriate behavior.

Debrief the Process

After students have participated in a structure or activity, spend a few minutes discussing the process, the successes, the challenges, and the outcomes. Since the goal is to both help students refine their skills and to deepen their content knowledge, ask students to reflect on what they learned, how they learned it, and what insights they had about their growth and knowledge. In addition, start doing some informal action research in your classroom. Based on feedback from students, keep notes about what was successful, what wasn't, and what adjustments might need to be made to ensure student success in the future.

Summary

Predominately silent, sedentary classrooms where students focus on individual tasks will not help them develop the skills necessary in the Common Core. In order for students to be college and career ready, they need to develop the ability to communicate with others through conversation, dialogue, and discussion. The ability to talk about learning not only helps students deepen content knowledge but it also helps them to develop essential 21st-Century skills.

Reflection Questions

1. As much as any other topic discussed throughout this book, the ability to have an in-depth and meaningful conversation is dependent upon a positive and supportive classroom culture. The atmosphere and relationships in the classroom must be supportive of conversation. Consider reviewing some of the topics from Chapters 1 and 2 to determine if any adjustments need to be made in order to increase the likelihood that students will engage in academic talk.

2. Mel Silberman, in his book *Active Learning—101 Strategies to Teach Any Subject,* says that, "Learning is not an automatic consequence of pouring information into a student's head." In what ways might this assumption be apparent in some classrooms?

3. Many of us have heard a variation of the expression *whoever does the teaching, does the learning.* If this expression has a ring of truth to it, what adjustments can be made to offer your students more opportunities to teach each other?

4. The importance of pre-planning was discussed in both Chapters 4 (Questioning) and 5 (Critical Thinking). What resources do you have at your disposal that can help with pre-planning academic conversations?

5. The three building blocks of effective student conversations are *curiosity, purpose,* and *structure.* Teachers have asked if all three elements are needed for every conversation. The answer is yes and no, depending on the students you serve. For some high-achieving, outgoing, and driven students you might only need a topic that piques their curiosity in order to get them talking. However, consider the needs of all the students you teach. How might the three building blocks support the needs of all students?

Extend Your Knowledge

- The book *Content-Area Conversations: How to Plan Discussion-Based Lessons for Diverse Language Learners* by Douglas Fisher, Nancy Frey and Carol Rothenberg provides useful tools and ideas for increasing student talk with a particular focus on diverse students and English Language learners.

- One of the best overall resources available on the topic of student conversation is the book *Academic Conversations* by Jeff Zwiers and Marie Crawford. It includes an excellent overview of the research that supports academic talk and includes useful tools and rubrics including a chapter on how to assess and grade student conversations.

- In the context of the classroom, the terms *conversation, dialogue,* and *discussion* are often used interchangeably. However, there are important differences. A conversation is an exchange of ideas, information, or opinions that is usually more relaxed and informal in nature. A dialogue is a more reflective process where the goal is to gain an understanding of another's point of view. Dialogue requires intentional listening, questioning, and reflecting in order to truly understand someone else's ideas. The goal of a discussion is to reach a decision. Sometimes thought of as an informal method of debate, a true discussion will lead to a conclusion or resolution of a problem or an issue.

- For a superb overview of the research that supports student talk read *Born to talk: An Introduction to Speech and Language Development* by Lloyd Hulit, Merle Howard, and Kathleen Fahey.

- A close read of the Standards for Mathematical Practice, which serve as a foundation for the Common Core Math Standards, will show direct and clear implications for student talk. In particular, Math Practice 3 states that students must, *Construct viable arguments and critique the reasoning of others.*

References

Allen, R. (2008). *Green Light Classrooms: Teaching Techniques That Acceler-ate Learning.* Thousand Oaks, CA: Corwin Press.

Alloway, T. P., & Alloway, R. G. (2010). Investigating the predictive roles of working memory and IQ in academic attainment. *Journal of Experimental Child Psychology,* 106(1), 20–9.

Arum, R., & Roksa, J. (2010). *Academically Adrift: Limited Learning on Col-lege Campuses.* Chicago, IL: University of Chicago Press.

Baumeister, R., & Tierney, J. (2012). *Willpower: Rediscovering the Greatest Human Strength.* New York: Penguin Books.

Bennett, S., & Kalish, N. (2007). *The Case Against Homework—How Home-work is Hurting Students and What Parents Can Do About It.* New York: Three Rivers Press.

Billmeyer, R., & Barton, M. L. (1998) *Teaching Reading in the Content Areas—If Not Me, Then Who?* Denver, CO: Mid-continent Research for Education and Learning.

Black, S. (2001). Ask me a question: How teachers use inquiry in the class-room. *American School Board Journal,* 188(5), 43–45.

Blackburn, B. (2008). *Rigor is NOT a Four-Letter Word.* Larchmont, NY: Eye On Education.

Breaux, A., & Whitaker, T. (2010). *50 Ways to Improve Student Behavior.* Larchmont, NY: Eye On Education.

Brualdi, Amy C. (1998). Classroom questions. *Practical Assessment, Research & Evaluation,* 6(6).

Burris, C., & Garrity, D. (2012). *Opening the Common Core.* Thousand Oaks, CA: Corwin Press.

Canady, R., & Rettig, M. (1996). *Teaching in the Block—Strategies for Engaging Active Learners.* Larchmont, NY: Eye On Education.

Charles, C. M. (2010). *Building Classroom Discipline.* New Jersey: Pearson.

Cooper, H. (2007). *The Battle Over Homework—Common Ground for Administrators, Teachers, and Parents.* Thousand Oaks, CA: Corwin Press.

Cotton, K. (1988). *Classroom Questioning.* School Improvement Research Series. Northwest Regional Educational Laboratory. http://educationnorthwest.org/webfm_send/569

Daniels, H. (2013). *Best Practice and the Common Core.* www.heinemann.com/pd/journal/Daniels_BestPractice_PDCJ_S13.pdf.

Darling-Hammond, L. (1997). *The Right to Learn—A Blueprint for Creating Schools that Work.* San Francisco: Jossey-Bass.

DePorter, B., Reardon, M., & Singer-Nourie, S. (1999). *Quantum Teaching: Orchestrating Student Success.* Boston: Allyn and Bacon.

Fisher, D., & Frey, N. (2007). *Checking for Understanding—Formative Assessment Techniques for Your Classroom.* Alexandria, VA: ASCD.

Fisher, D., Frey, N., & Lapp, D. (2011) *Teaching Students to Read Like Detectives.* Bloomington, IN: Solution Tree.

Fisher, D., Frey, N., & Lapp, D. (2012) *Text Complexity—Raising Rigor in Reading.* Newark, DE: International Reading Association.

Fisher, D., Frey, N., & Rothenberg, C. (2008). *Content-Area Conversations: How to Plan Discussion-Based Lessons for Diverse Language Learners.* Alexandria, VA: ASCD.

Florez, I. (2011). Developing Young Children's Self-Regulation Skills through Everyday Experiences. *Young Children.* July 2011.

Gregory, G., & Chapman, C. (2002). *Differentiated Instructional Strategies: One Size Doesn't Fit All.* Thousand Oaks, CA: Corwin Press.

Guskey, T. (Ed.). (2006). *Benjamin Bloom—Portraits of an Educator.* Lanham, Maryland: Rowman & Littlefield Education.

Harris, B., & Goldberg, C. (2012). *75 Quick and Easy Solutions to Common Classroom Disruptions.* Larchmont, NY: Eye On Education.

Hattie, J. (2008). *Visible Learning: A Synthesis of Over 800 Meta-Analyses Relating to Achievement.* New York: Routledge.

Heath, C., & Heath, D. (2008). *Made to Stick.* New York: Random House.

Hulit, L. M., Howard, M. R., & Fahey, K. R. (2010). *Born to Talk: An Introduction to Speech and Language Development.* Boston, MA: Allyn & Bacon International Center for Leadership in Education. http://www.leadered.com/pdf/R&Rframework.pdf

Jackson, R. (2010). *Never Work Harder than Your Students and Other Principles of Great Teaching.* Alexandria, VA: ASCD.

Jensen, E. (2000). *Brain-Based Learning.* San Diego, CA: The Brain Store.

Jensen, E. (2005). *Teaching with the Brain in Mind.* Alexandria, VA: ASCD.

Jensen, E. (2012). *Self-Control Made Easy.* Brighter Brain Bulletin.

Johnson, B. (2012). *Teaching Students to Dig Deeper—The Common Core in Action.* Larchmont, NY: Eye On Education.

Jones, F. (2007). *Tools for Teaching.* Santa Cruz, CA: Fred Jones and Associates

Kohn, A. (1999). *Punished by Rewards.* New York: Houghton Mifflin.

Kohn, A. (2007). *The Homework Myth: Why Our Kids Get Too Much of a Bad Thing.* Boston, MA: Da Capo Press.

Lavoie, R. (2007). *The Motivation Breakthrough: 6 Secrets to Turning on the Tuned-Out Child.* New York, NY: Touchstone.

Lehrer, J. (2009). Don't—The Secret of Self-Control. *New Yorker Magazine.*

Marzano, R. (2007). *The Art and Science of Teaching.* Alexandria, VA: ASCD.

Marzano, R., Pickering, D., & Pollock, J. (2001). *Classroom Instruction that Works: Research- Based Strategies for Increasing Student Achievement.* Alexandria, VA: ASCD.

Medina, J. (2008). *Brain Rules—12 Principles for Surviving and Thriving at Work, Home, and School.* Seattle, WA: Pear Press.

Mendler, A. (2001) *Connecting with Students.* Alexandria, VA: ASCD

Mischel, W., Shoda, Y., & Rodriguez, M. (1989). Delay of gratification in children. *Science, 244,* 933–938.

Moffitt, T. et al. (2011). A gradient of childhood self-control predicts health, wealth, and public Safety. Department of Psychology, Duke University, Durham, NC.

National Governors Association Center for Best Practices, Council of Chief State School Officers (2010). *Common Core State Standards.* Washington DC: National Governors Association Center for Best Practices, Council of Chief State School Officers.

National Research Council. (2000). *How People Learn.* Washington, DC: National Academy Press.

Oregon Small Schools Initiative, http://www.e3smallschools.org/ar.html.

Pollock, J. (2011) *Feedback: The Hinge that Joins Teaching and Learning.* Thousand Oaks, CA: Corwin.

Reif, S. (2003). *The ADHD Book of Lists.* San Francisco, CA: Josey Bass.

Roth, L. (2012). *Brain-Powered Strategies to Engage All Learners.* Oceanside, CA: Shell Education

Shanahan, T. (2012). *What is Close Reading?* www.shanahanonliteracy.com/2012/06/what-is-close-reading.html (last accessed February 2013).

Silberman, M. (1996). *Active Learning—101 Strategies to Teach Any Subject.* Needham Heights, MA: Allyn & Bacon.

Stahl, R. (1994). *Using Wait Time and Think Time Skillfully in the Classroom.* http://www.ericdigests.org/1995–1/think.htm (last accessed February 2013).

Tovani, C. (2000). *I Read It, but I Don't Get It—Comprehension Strategies for Adolescent Readers.* Portland, ME: Stenhouse Publishers.

Wagner, T. (2008). Rigor Redefined. *Educational Leadership, 66,* 20–25.

Walsh, J., & Sattes, B. (2005). *Quality Questioning: Research-Based Practice to Engage Every Learner.* Thousand Oask, CA: Corwin Press.

Willis, J. (2007). *Brain-Friendly Strategies for the Inclusion Classroom.* Alexandria, VA: ASCD.

Willingham, D. (2009). *Why Don't Students Like School?* San Francisco: Josey-Bass.

Zwiers, J., & Crawford, M. (2011). *Academic Conversations—Classroom Talk that Fosters Critical Thinking and Content Understandings.* Portland, ME: Stenhouse Publishers.